GOD AT GROUND LEVEL

God at Ground Level

RALPH CAPENERHURST
AND EDDY STRIDE

FALCON BOOKS · LONDON

First published 1972
Copyright © Ralph Capenerhurst 1972
SBN 85491 525 7

The quotation from the New English Bible
is by courtesy of the Oxford and
Cambridge University Presses.

FALCON BOOKS
are published by CPAS Publications, a department of
the Church Pastoral Aid Society,
Falcon Court, 32 Fleet Street, London ECY 1DB

Overseas Agents
Emu Book Agencies Ltd
511 Kent Street, Sydney, NSW, Australia

CSSM and Crusader Bookroom Society Ltd
177 Manchester Street, Christchurch, New Zealand

Sunday School Centre Wholesale
PO Box 3020, Cape Town, South Africa

Contents

Foreword	7
1. Time to Clock On	9
2. The Cell	15
3. The Awkward Squad	25
4. All Out	33
5. A Question of Colour	42
6. Out on the Fringe	49
7. Snap	58
8. The Hard Cases	71
Epilogue	89
Commentary and questions for discussion	93

Foreword

This is a sketch of the Church witnessing and working for Christ on the workshop floor.

The Christian in industry is increasingly subjected to the pressures of secularism and the materialistic philosophy which naturally evolves. In this book I have attempted to describe some of the pressures: a few of these stem from official – managerial and union – level, some from unofficial minority groups and some from the simple fact that man is basically sinful.

The railway industry, comparatively speaking, has maintained a clean bill of health as far as official and unofficial strikes are concerned and a traditional humanitarianism has acted as a brake against the excesses, such as kangaroo courts, so prevalent in other unions.

Throughout the story I have described the Christian community on the shop floor as 'the Cell'. There is, of course, a sinister Communistic connotation in the use of this term but if it implies a closely-knit community working together for a common purpose, this is exactly what is happening.

I am aware of the deficiencies in this type of reporting. A trained observer would probably interpret life on the shop floor in a totally different way and for the reader who prefers a more erudite study, H.F.R. Catherwood's *The Christian in Industrial Society* (Tyndale Press, 1964) is an obvious choice.

For obvious reasons I have compounded certain characters

and chronologically displaced events, but the personalities and situations are drawn from real life.

I am grateful to the Rev. Eddy Stride for adding an illuminating thought-provoking commentary to the story.

Ralph Capenerhurst

1. Time to Clock On

For twenty-odd years I have punched a clocking machine; for almost four thousand days excluding annual and public holidays; I have had what some people would call a regular rat race from the council estate where I live to the British Rail workshops where I work. The Depot employs some four thousand men and they are engaged in making and repairing BR rolling stock.

I am familiar with the smells of my calling: creosote, cutting oil, resin and burning diesel oil – all offend the senses. The noises too; the ear-splitting shriek of metal on metal in the erecting shop, the mighty hammers in the drop-forge, the defening nightmare of the guns that batter corroding scars of rust off metal girders, the deafening roar of the accumulator house and the giant boiler plant.

As a labourer, I have the opportunity of observing life from the lowest layer of the industrial stratum. Some men do this in a literal sense as their job consists in cleaning out the pits beneath the drilling and planing machines. This is uncongenial work where one's clothes become saturated with evil-smelling 'suds', the stuff used for cooling the metal as it is being 'worked'. Other labourers unload incoming wagons of buffers and axleboxes and suchlike, others dig out trenches and carve out footings in the general repair and maintenance of the plant which is a huge complex sprawling over many acres in the industrial heart of the city.

A smoke-pall perpetually veils the area where I work. Chimneys belch out the afterbirth of things metallic so that a fine black powder is deposited all over the place – the Smoke Abatement Society hasn't got round to the problem yet. The metal mountains in the near distance are full of gas and the atmosphere is heavily charged with the offending smell. It is alarming to see the dust drifting to earth when the sun breaks through the swirling smoke. Eyes, nose, mouth – not to mention the lungs – get clogged with dust. However, adequate provision is made for one to walk out fresh and clean after a shift for the amenity blocks incorporate every modern convenience. At strategic points in the works there are slot machines where milk, hot coffee, chocolates and cigarettes may be purchased at any time of day. Even the men's leisure time has the BR stamp upon it for organized recreational facilities cater for every interest and hobby.

At about eight-thirty the salaried staff arrive, and the shop staff who began their working day an hour earlier resent what they feel is an artificial class distinction. The labourers engaged in yard duties whistle at the pretty office girls who blushingly refuse to respond to their calls. The young male clerks in their Harris Tweed jackets and buffed leather sleeves hurry by ignoring the mean glances and crisp asides from the labouring fraternity who take any opportunity to bait them. The fact that the salaried staff work under better conditions with fringe benefits acts as an abrasive, continually chafing the sensitive disposition on the shop-floor employees.

But the office staff have their problems; 'I don't see Mr Smith or Miss Roberts walking along the corridor,' confessed one of the clerks to me the other day, 'I just see a *grade*' and in this one pregnant sentence lies the soullessness of the whole industrial scene – in spite of those glass and concrete amenity blocks. Everyone is aware that the increase in technology brings problems for the human personality. This is felt not only at office and shop-floor level but is also sensed in management. We are living in the overlap of great changes on the industrial and social front and the problems that confront us are essentially human and moral and are problems for resolving in the Church rather than the Boardroom.

Even on the shop floor there is a three-tier social strata – the unskilled labourer, the semi-skilled bench-hand and the skilled worker. There is a subtle snobbery in the overall brigade. The skilled worker is jealous of his craft; he is the aristocrat of the shop floor and commands a high pay packet for his undoubted skill. Having served a long apprenticeship on a low rate of pay he is probably entitled to a certain measure of respect from his technically inferior workmates. This attitude often acts as an abrasive on his lower-paid colleague who is the fetcher and carrier, the putter-up and lifter-down of the working partnership. When a force five east wind whistles down the long lines of gaunt workshops and the rain cuts into the exposed flesh like a thousand needles, it is the labourer who is told by the chargehand millwright to fetch a couple of gallons of cutting oil from the oil store. Again, the unskilled man is part of the labour pool and where mobility of manpower are the chief criteria for getting a job done in a hurry, there is always an underlying impermanence surrounding any job the labourer happens to be doing.

The craftsman whose skills are about to be swallowed up in the maw of automation; the bench-hand whose assistance will no longer be needed; the labourer who chucks lumps of iron into railway wagons for a living – as a missionary to industry, this is my parish and these are my problems.

There is a multiplicity of bosses and they come in all shapes and sizes. The upper-strata men are rarely seen on the shop floor except when some visiting dignitaries are being shown around the works. The edicts and instructions from 'Top Office' percolate through a variety of departments to the workshop.

Descending the managerial ladder, the terminal point of authority is reached at the shop-floor foreman. He is a much troubled man who bears everyone's burden – production, planning, progress, stores – the lot. All departments coalesce in him. Usually he has worked his way up to the foreman's office via the shop floor and is therefore familiar with the restrictive practices and minor misdemeanours of the shop-floor fraternity. He has a first-name relationship with the older hands and although he does not condone the practices in which he himself formerly indulged – clocking someone else's card for example – he ensures he is not around when it is done. If he is obliged to warn a man his tone is muted by the ever-present threat that the offender might with a leer reply, 'Look 'ere Bill, – you used to clock your mates in when you was on the floor'. The most successful foreman I know refers to a man by his surname and prefixes it with 'Mr'. He takes decisions and acts with initiative and imagination. He does not go 'a-slumming' with his men – indulging in loose ribaldry and being awfully embarrassed in the process. He earns respect rather than asks for it and the welfare of his men is a prime consideration. He is quite frank in his declared intention of 'getting on' and the goodwill of the men under him will boost his personal stock because he'll get the job done quicker and more efficiently with a happy and balanced labour force.

Among the men, it is a stock joke and one with more than a grain of truth that, prior to the start of the Second World War, foremen were 'made' not within the confines of the works but rather in the sanctified cloisters of the Church – St Botolph's to be precise. St Botolph's is near to the works and has always been regarded as the Railway Church. Many years ago the sidesmen, choir members and wardens – indeed, anyone who had a part to play in the life of St Botolph's – were employed by the London Midland and Scottish Railway Company. A kind of spiritual nepotism prevailed and plum jobs were reserved for the fraternity who worshipped within the hallowed walls of St Botolph's.

The older hands have not forgotten these times and with a schizophrenic disregard for logic, attribute the current 'couldn't care less' attitude (which they deplore) to the slackness in discipline that has occurred since the railways were nationalized, while at the same time applauding the slot machines and amenity blocks which have only come because 'we fought for our rights'. 'Nowadays' they say, 'foremen are made in the "Angry Saracen" ' (a local pub). This sort of reasoning might be interesting to a social 'engineer'! One is frequently reminded of the dark genesis of a supervisor's position by a crafty allusion to 'his dad was in St Botolph's choir!' and somehow, Christianity is related to these discredited practices of a past generation.

It is not always easy for the outsider to understand the different mental attitudes between those who simply *have* a job and those who *follow* a career. There is a subtle blockage in the aspirations of the factory worker engaged on some soul-destroying task. He lives in a society geared to planned obsolescence and material prosperity and it is no wonder that his mental horizons extend no further than the Friday wage packet and knocking-off time.

Too often, there is little sense of pride and achievement, where the de-humanizing element of the man with the stopwatch is seen as the chief factor in determining wage rates. It may be that some of the wildcat strikes that have bedevilled the industrial scene are really unconscious cries for attention: cries for recognition that man is mightier than the assembly line. Looked at in this context, this is a hopeful sign. It is true that some individuals prefer a job which calls for no imagination and is repetitive. But this is something which we must acknowledge as a blot on our society for it strikes at the roots of what a man *is*. The Christian on the factory floor recognizes that his workmate is an individual and has a creative intelligence.

Many old hands are keenly disappointed at what they feel is the declining need for the old, traditional skills and standards of craftsmanship. But can it be that the Rolls Royce collapse may be partly attributed to superb standards without reference to a competitive market and obsolescence as a way of life?

It is against such a backdrop where the whole fabric of our industrial life and thinking has changed that the Christian seeks to influence his fellow workmates and lead them into a knowledge of Him who offers abundant life.

2. The Cell

Bert Stalker is a squat, little man. He has large sad St Bernard-like eyes and a pugnacious jaw. His appearance is heralded by a strong smell of diesel gas oil colloquially known as 'Blue Billy'. Veiling the bald patch on his head he wears a cap, the design of which has long since disappeared beneath a dozen layers of grease accumulated during its lengthy life. Bert also wears a large apron which commences at his neck and terminates at his ankles. Needless to say the well-greased apron could very well remain in a vertical position unsupported!

Bert belongs to the group of Christians in what we call 'the Cell', and he is a 'fundamental evangelical full-gospel-no-nonsense' Christian. He works as a labourer in a piecework gang. Bert is strong as an elephant, patient as an ox and courageous as a lion, but there is nothing bovine about Bert's attitude towards life. His mates call him 'the Vicar' and Bert bears this nickname with fitting dignity.

There are a few men in the rail-yard who knew Bert in his pre-conversion days and they have a distinct respect for him. 'There was a time,' says one 'when if you knocked on Bert's door you were likely to stop a bunch of fives before a word was exchanged.' 'I remember when he was starting up his haulage business in the twenties,' says another, 'he lopped his lorry down to conform to what he considered was a reasonable size – insurance-wise – and then he secured a contract to cart bricks. He tried to take two loads in one hop and was halfway up Cemetery Hill when the middle of his cut-down lorry buckled and broke in two and ten thousand bricks spilled out all over the road!'

Bert's conversion was sudden, dramatic and accompanied by a powerful emotional response. During the thirties when times were hard, Bert, with two million others, was out of a job. He had only been married a short time and was feeling the pinch.

Bert and his wife, Sue, lived in a mean little house in Billow Row and although Sue worked her fingers to the bone trying to keep the place neat and tidy, the walls still exuded moisture and the dank odour from the drains still clogged the atmosphere. These conditions were a breeding ground for discontent and quarrels and splits in family life. One night, disconsolate and dejected, he was walking past the Ebenezer Mission Hall and spilling out into the night came the strains of 'count your many blessings' – complete with tambourines! Bert repressed a rueful smile – blessings indeed! But the lights in the Mission Hall were inviting and it was warm in there so he stepped over the threshold intending to stand in the vestibule and just listen.

'Welcome brother, it's good to see you! Will you accept a hymn book? Thank you! – now, this way . . . ' and Bert, hardly knowing what was happening was gently but firmly propelled into the body of the hall and seated on a chair. He looked around and his normally courageous heart suddenly began to tremble with a strange fear. All the people were *singing,* some were clapping in time with the music and someone was calling him 'Brother' and shaking his hand. Bert had never thought people could be *happy* singing *hymns*!

Then a man stood up on the raised dais at the front of the hall and began to preach, not in the well-oiled tones of what Bert firmly believed were the hallmark of the paid professional but in the rough, uncultured speech of Billow Row.

'You 'ain't right wiv God! Before you leave this place tonight you've *got* to get right 'n' there's only one way,' and here he stabbed his finger in Bert's direction. 'You've got to come to Christ because you're a sinner 'n' God 'ates sin, but Jesus died for all sinners on the cross; you *must* be born again!' The words seemed to thud convulsively into Bert's consciousness.

16

'For the first time in my life, I knew that God loved me,' Bert says reflectively 'and when the preacher asked us to signify our acceptance of salvation my hand shot up like a rocket!' Spontaneously the congregation began to sing

> 'Ring the bells of Heaven,
> There is joy today,
> For a soul returning from the wild,
> See the Father meets him out upon the way,
> Welcoming His weary, wandering child . . . '

and Bert knew there was joy in heaven!

Afterwards he was counselled by the preacher who gave him a New Testament and invited him to come the following night and bring his wife. It was a strange joy, intoxicating and heady, yet Bert knew that his experience was real. *Something* wonderful had truly happened to him. He hurried home and announced to Sue that he was 'saved' and she, not understanding the depth of his experience, agreed to accompany him the following night, where she underwent a similar transformation.

Bill and Sue were rapidly integrated into the life of Bethesda Mission. In those days there was no set time for finishing the meetings. The New Testament spirit of fellowship was communicated to the hearts of these simple folk. They prayed together, sang together, shared each other's burdens and trials and wept together. 'The Meeting' was the focal point in this couple's life, the watershed of all their hopes and aspirations. There the Bible was expounded, the gospel proclaimed, and the 'songs of Zion' sung.

Bert has known no other form of worship nor involved himself in any other aspect of the Church's life and activity other than that promoted by Bethesda Mission. He is suspicious of a liturgical form of service feeling that it somehow chokes the activity of the Holy Spirit and binds the worshipper to a man-made format of legality and stifling discipline.

His simple directness is often more successful in personal witness than a reasoned, studied approach. When a man blasphemes in his presence, Bert immediately takes him to task. 'You are taking my Saviour's name in vain. He died on the cross for me – and you – and I strongly object to you using His name in this way.' I have never known this devastating rejoinder to fail, for it is delivered in an uncommonly authoritative tone. Hard men have blustered and stumbled in their reactions to this verbal broadside but all have been subdued and subsequently bridled their tongues in Bert's presence.

Insular to some degree and at times condescending to other members of the Cell who own to a liturgical form of worship. Bert is a walking concordance of Scripture texts. He shuns argument and discussion which is not solely concerned with spiritual matters, feeling that it is 'unprofitable' and this creates an impression of stand-offishness to the men with whom he is working. This mental monasticism naturally imposes a rather naïve outlook on world affairs. Social responsibility is something quite alien to Bert's concept of the Christian's role in the world. Nevertheless, he is a man of strong principles who is prepared to state categorically *what* he believes and *why* he believes. There are many chameleon-like characters who shed their respectability once they are within the factory gates. Bert, notwithstanding his eccentricities, is useful ballast in our Christian community.

Another person in the Cell is Tom Slaney, the Church of England member of our fraternity. I have a special affection for Tom for he first introduced me to local preaching and stood by me at my first attempts to preach in the open air.

Tom was born into a family of nine – four brothers and five sisters. In the days of the depression, the district where he lived had a notorious reputation and even the police patrolled the area in two's and three's on Saturday nights after the pubs had closed.

Tom's father was an alcoholic and many were the nights when the whole family was subjected to the crazy actions of his besotted brain. Sometimes, he would bring his boozy companions into the small terraced house and then the table would be literally strewed with beer and spirits and the night would be punctuated with obscenities and lewd songs. Not that this was unusual in the district but Tom remembers those nights and the brutalizing effect they had on him.

His father's working life had been spent as a labourer in the rail-yard – except for a four year spell during the depression when, like millions more, he was sacked. It was during those bleak and bitter years that Tom's mother would go to the local market place late on Saturday nights. In the winter the winds would whip and snap at the canvas covers of the stalls as meat and vegetables were sold off at bargain prices. Those were the days when 'specs' from the greengrocer's were eagerly seized upon by Tom and his pals and carried home in triumph. After the bad and mouldy parts of the fruit were cut away, the rest was wholesome and good and all the family enjoyed the pickings. Stale cakes were also a treat, although one had to get up early and be first at the confectioner's in order to obtain the chocolate eclairs and vanilla slices. The cream was slightly 'off', but Tom recalls a wonderful glow of joyful extravagance as he sank his teeth into a frothy cream horn – unmindful of any imperfections in the flavour.

Tom grew up with a built-in acceptance of certain values. The 'Robin Hood', the 'Angry Saracen', and 'The George', were the normal places where one sought social pleasure. True, the evangelical parish church of St Saviour's came round the district with a band of zealots and a wheezy portable organ on Sunday nights and Tom, with a rueful smile of self-reproach, remembers how some of the 'specs', pappy and mouldering, were used for a quite unworthy purpose . . .

A few months before the Second World War broke out, when Tom was working in the rail-yard, he joined the local branch of the 'Terry's' – the Territorial Army. There was a useful bounty and two weeks training away from the meanness of his home district in the rolling Welsh hills. When war was de-clared, Tom, along with other members of his family, soon found himself called up for active service and within a few weeks, he landed in France.

'We're gonna hang out the washing on the Siegfried Line
Have you any dirty washing mother dear . . . '

'Run rabbit, run rabbit, run, run, run,
. . . you'll get by, without your rabbit pie,
So run rabbit, run rabbit, run, run, run.'

Tom remembers well the familiar songs of that period of the 'phoney war' for it was during one of the singing sessions in the NAAFI canteen that they received the unbelievable order to retreat. The war was phoney no longer. The German armies scythed across Europe compressing the Allied troops into a tight and exposed group on the Dunkirk beaches. Many of Tom's friends were killed during the initial stages of retreat. German Stukas continually dive-bombed the narrow country road jammed with Allied troops and machine-gunned the fleeing civilian refugees. Tom was on the beaches three days and two nights before being picked up by one of the small boats in that heroic armada that was hastily assembled to extricate the remnants of the BEF.

'That was the first time I was convinced that the folk from St Saviour's had the edge on mine host at the "Angry Saracen"!' says Tom. 'The sea was like a millpond and the weather held until the operation was over. I saw the *Lancastria* go down and saw things and heard things I shall never forget . . . and I was sure God had His hand upon me . . . '

Tom spent the rest of the war as a Royal Artillery gunner on board merchant vessels and travelled all over the world. Amazingly, he passed through many U-boat infested waters in convoy but never once was the ship on which he happened to be serving attacked.

After the war was over, Tom took up the threads of civilian life again and went back to his old job as a labourer in the rail-yard. There he met a young man, George, who had also returned from the wars and was a convinced Christian. There was something about him that Tom could not understand; he was so *sure* about the truth of Christianity. One sentence which George almost casually dropped in conversation lodged in Tom's mind: 'I believe God has His hand upon you, Tom' he had said. Somehow, in spite of the fact that Tom had taken up his old life – the pub crawls, the doubtful companions, the meaningless ritual of the daily grind at the rail-yard – Tom felt that his life was moving towards a climax. It was all so strange, so intangible and yet the truth of what George had said to him during those lunch breaks was inescapable. Tom *knew* that God was calling him.

'Do you mind if I come to church with you next Sunday?' he asked one day over 'snap'. There was a gleam in George's eye, 'I'd welcome your company!' he said.

They went to a small independent mission hall. The service took the usual form and the minister, presumably recognizing that Tom was a stranger in the meeting, preached fervently on 'The Brazen Serpent' – and he preached for a decision.

At the end of his address, he asked the congregation to bow their heads and invited anyone who felt their need of the Lord Jesus Christ to raise their hand. Tom felt very self-conscious – yet strangely unsettled. The hall was stuffy and he was embarrassed by the spontaneous outbursts of the people praying around him. George seemed to be caught up in the spirit of the meeting and Tom was very relieved when the pastor asked the congregation to sit up, and he announced the last hymn.

After the benediction, George escorted Tom to the exit where the minister was shaking hands with the departing congregation. Tom halted for a moment as the pastor gripped his hand. 'Are you a Christian?' he asked in an imperious, yet kindly tone. Tom could not answer for the words seemed to be hurtling in on his mind from a vast distance. He only knew that this was the moment when God required him to act decisively: he was a sinner and the way of salvation had been clearly stated. Almost instinctively, he sank to his knees in the doorway leading from the church hall into the street and he was joined by the minister, his friend George, and the rest of the people. Something dynamic had happened in Tom's experience and as the pastor prayed, he knew he was a *different* man. Tom has become a convinced Calvinist since his conversion – 'It's a revelation!' he says when he is challenged by Bert on this point.

All this happened almost twenty years ago and George, God's 'middle-man', has since left the railway service. Tom did not make his spiritual 'home' at the mission but joined his local parish church, St Saviour's. It had been this church which sought his spiritual good when he was a young boy. Now happily married, with a Christian wife and three sons, he is like the man in Psalm 16: 'The lines have fallen for me in pleasant places' he says.

Bert and Tom are typical of those who make up the Cell, dedicated, dependable – the old guard. It is largely their generation who make up the group, although there is a sprinkling of younger men. Their IQ's may not be outstanding but they are the kind of men God uses for a distinctive witness on the workshop floor. The Berts and Toms have been tested in all kinds of situations calculated to inspire fear or embarrassment in a sensitive heart. At various times they have been ostracized by the men, caricatured and ridiculed but, on rare occasions, they have received the applause of their workmates for their courage in standing for the truth as they see it. It is a privilege to shoulder one's Christian responsibilities alongside such sterling characters.

We were busy shifting desks and chairs into the new office-block when I met Jim; he was signwriting on the various departmental doors, quietly engrossed in his task and very softly whistling a familiar hymn-tune. I signalled to my mate to lower his end of the heavy desk we were carrying and then did likewise. I walked over to Jim, 'Do you know what you are whistling?' I enquired with a quizzical smile. Without turning his head he answered, 'Yes, do you?'

'Yes, tell me, are you a Christian?'

'I am and have been for almost forty years. I am a *born-again* Christian!'

He laid down his brush, turned his head and fixed me with a pair of clear blue eyes, 'Are you born again?' he asked quietly.

'Oh yes, I was converted while serving in the army, in Palestine, 1946.'

'You've been to Palestine?' he said. 'Tell me, what was it like? Did you manage to visit most of the biblical places . . . ?'

That was my first introduction to Jim, an elite tradesman, a craftsman of the old school who took a real pride in the job and a Christian of sterling worth.

Jim identified himself with the Cell when time and opportunity afforded. He was a member of the Open Brethren but lamented that the spiritual tone of assembly life these days was somewhat lower than that of former years. Like Bert, he knew the Bible well and could recite the entire Epistle of Paul to the Romans off by heart! He was pre-eminent in his role of Bible teaching and I arranged a winter session of Bible studies in my home in order that we all might profit from his unique ministry. This was the start of the house meetings which were always well attended and very lively!

Jim had been transferred to Moortown from Manchester many years before and although he had not experienced the bitter poverty and unemployment of the 'Evil Thirties', he had been subjected to the harsh pressures of militant trade unionism on account of his conscientious objection to joining the union. Before 'kangaroo courts' made their infamous appearance on the British industrial scene or the Industrial Relations Bill was mooted, Jim had suffered the appalling misery of being 'sent to Coventry' for a lengthy spell.

Unless one has experienced the sense of isolation, the feeling of being a moral outcast among one's fellows, it is difficult to describe the dreadful circumstances in which one must go about the everyday task of earning a living. Men have suffered mental

23

breakdowns, others have committed suicide when militant extremists have used this beastly method to secure their selfish ends. Jim never joined a trade union and the men alongside whom he worked never forgot. In an industrial dispute where a strike might be threatened, old men with selective memories will always breathe 'blackleg' when the name of a nonconformist with strong convictions against strike action is mentioned. 'Blackleg' is the dirtiest word in shop-floor jargon – much dirtier than the dirtiest four letter word. Yet in spite of such pressures Jim had stood his ground.

3. The Awkward Squad

'Like a mighty army . . .' and in every army there are the platoons with an awkward squad. They seem to have a congenital disability to distinguish their right hand from their left, they march out of step and clumsily drop their rifles on the Queen's Birthday Parade . . . we in the workshops also have an 'awkward squad'. On the whole the rest of the Cell are charitably disposed to these brethren. Sometimes we feel they are the whetstone on which our grace and patience are sharpened, for while we are answerable for our individual testimonies we are also identified with each other. There are no rabbinical schools of learning and our corporate doctrine must preserve and present a measure of uniformity. The slightest deviation from accepted evangelical principles is eagerly seized upon by the men and exhibited as evidence that 'Christians can't agree among themselves'. Bert's suspicion of Tom and his churchy attitude must therefore never be voiced in the company of the rest of the labouring gang; Tom's doubts about the effervescent quality of Fred's 'baptism in the Holy Spirit' and his 'speaking in tongues' is likewise suffocated. Doctrinal differences among ourselves however are freely aired and generally debated in a charitable atmosphere.

Occasionally, one of the awkward squad will fracture the image of Christian unity. A careless word, an outburst of temper, a doctrinal hobby-horse which he must mount in public – while we are all vulnerable to such failings, some are more vulnerable than others. Therefore, the Christian must not only learn to conduct affairs with the nonchristians on the shop floor, he must also accommodate the vagaries of the awkward squad. After a while, he may reach the conclusion that at their best, they are unpredictable and at their worst, unbearable, but in the final analysis, the Christian who is out of step is the brother for whom Christ died and he must be treated on that basis.

The early church had its awkward squad. James and John, the Sons of Thunder, overtly ambitious for the first place in the Kingdom and hardly likely to inspire confidence in the outsider who might have heard them discussing plans to raze a village simply because of its inhospitality; Peter – blind, loveable, impetuous, questioning – and seriously out of step with His Master's plans on the slopes of Caesarea Phillipi; Judas, a dark and lonely incarnation of evil; Euodias and Syntyche, the squabbling sisters of Phillipi; Diotrephes who wanted to be 'top dog'; the partisan groups at Corinth . . . The manifold grace of God, redeeming and restoring, enabled those who availed themselves of its transforming power to overcome their limitations and defects; that selfsame grace also enabled their fellow-believers to put up with them in the process!

So, on the workshop floor we must exercise a charitable patience and not a little humour when the odd quirks of our brethren in Christ seem seriously to jar on our nerves or offend our sensitivity.

The discipline of local church life contains these folk but when they are in a workshop environment and regarded by the men – quite rightly – as Christ's representatives, then their statements and actions may sometimes cause an anxious frown on the brow of the saint and a cynical grin on the lips of the unconverted sinner! The man who has a stoppage in the brain regarding blood and black puddings and never tires of advancing scriptural reasons to support his pet views; the otherwise orthodox fellow believer who continually harps on Daniel's Seventieth Week in a B-flat voice quivering like a cello string; the man who habitually uses the 'language of Zion' before his uncomprehending workmates; these men are not regarded as cranks in their local churches but they are certainly looked upon as odd in the workshop.

Take Sam Blarney for example. Sam belonged to our fraternity before his retirement. In his younger days, Sam had been a professional boxer but ruefully admitted that he wasn't a very good one. His pugilistic career had left him physically handicapped, which was manifested in a nervous twitching of his right eye, that made him appear to be constantly winking. This caused him acute embarrassment especially when there were young ladies in the vicinity! He was once detailed to clean the new boss's window and began the task in his usual zealous manner. After a while, the boss sent for the chargehand. 'Will you please ask that man who is cleaning my windows to refrain? I've said "Good morning" to him a dozen times already!'

Sam was held in high repute by the men. They ragged him unmercifully about his boxing prowess – or lack of it. It was a popular joke that 'Sam has a wicked right and his left isn't much better'. It was widely rumoured that once after Sam had swiped at an opponent and missed him the adversary had died of pneumonia.

When he joined the ambulance classes to learn first aid, Sam's twitch occasioned many jokes. It was rumoured that one day he bandaged up someone's left arm instead of the right index finger. It was further unkindly suggested that should one be so unfortunate as to be revived by the kiss of life from Sam, one would die of shock anyway . . .

Sam never complained about any job he was detailed to perform, so he was therefore the first port of call for any hard-pressed chargehand who wanted a man to do a dirty job in a hurry. He was always cheerful but his besetting sin was that he was easily provoked in an argument. Sporting topics usually provided the bait. The gang would introduce a controversial note in a mock-argument among themselves and Sam would prick up his ears.

'Jimmy Wilde had the fastest punch ever – that's official!'

'That's a flat lie – the record's held by Carnera'; and Sam, quietly enough, would attempt to put the matter right: 'Say lads, the record is held by Sugar Ray Robinson – 35 m.p.h. I think; January '57 he did it!' and this was the signal for the rest of the gang to shout him down.

'Shurrup Sam – you know now't about it!'

'You're talking daft, again, Sam!'

'Be quiet! – you're all wrong, I *know* you're wrong!' Sam would howl, his face set in an aggressive snarl and his eyes blazing with indignation. His agitation would increase as he attempted to make his point and he would breathe heavily in an attempt to control his feelings but as the storm subsided, he would twitch uncontrollably.

His Christian witness was hardly ever treated seriously by the men. They regarded his almost fanatical interest in boxing and his fidelity to the Christian faith as a curious anomaly. They patronized him, gave him the left-overs from their 'snap-bags' and watched him hungrily devour the sardine rolls and bread and dripping sandwiches.

Deliberately, they used him as a butt for their often twisted sense of humour. 'Hey, Sam, come here, here's a good, clean joke . . . ' and Sam, completely naïve, would cock his ear while they rapidly trundled out a stream of obscenities. With an almost bovine acceptance of his lot, Sam carried on, convinced that at the end of life's road, a crown awaited him in heaven . . .

Of course, other members of the Christian fraternity attempted to counsel and advise him not to be drawn into any arguments and refrain from giving the gang an opportunity to take a rise out of him but somehow Sam saw his self-imposed martyrdom as a short cut to that heavenly crown.

The Sam's are found in every Christian community. Un-complaining, hardworking, they set up the tables and chairs for the Sunday School parties, take a hand on the bookstall at the missionary rallies, help to sort out the children on the annual Sunshine Corner rambles, roll up their sleeves when the church needs a spring clean . . . they belong to the vast army of unknowns who make up the great body of the Christian Church.

Bob is also categorized in the awkward squad. He is a 'witnesser'. He believes in witnessing to *five* people every day – anywhere, anytime, anybody – but the number must be five. 'Five' has assumed a mystical significance in Bob's mind. He is a lanky six-footer with a look of complete abjection, but this forbidding exterior veils a very sprightly and gay personality. Bob has a highly individual approach to the problem of breaking down all resistance to personal Christian witness. After settling on his quarry, Bob will screw up his mouth rather after the manner of those old American movie gangsters and enquire, 'What church 'ave I seen you at?'

'You ain't seen me at any church!' might be the prickly reply.

'Why ain't I?'

' 'Cos I don't believe in it!'

'Why don't you believe in it?' Bob will doggedly persist.

'Because it ain't true.'

'Who sez?'

'I say.'

Bob will try a new tack. 'You're a sinner!'

' 'N' you are!' is the quick rejoinder.

'Yes, but Jesus died on the cross so we could be saved. The Bible says, "The soul that sinneth, it shall die" and if you ain't saved, you'll die . . . '

'Ain't you going to die?'

'Yes. But when I die I'll go to be with Jesus in 'eaven but if you die *unsaved – you'll go to 'ell*!' – and the almost brutally frank manner in which this undoubtedly sound advice is volunteered, coupled with the hushed and awesome tone of Bob's voice, has caused strong men to blanch. After Bob has unloaded his rather weighty theological proposition on to his quarry's worried mind, he will straighten up. 'Ah well,' he will say in a considerably lighter tone, 'you ain't my responsibility now, I've put you right and now it's up to you!' and he departs, sometimes leaving the man with a puzzled look on his face and mixed emotions in his heart. More often, he goes with hoots of ribald laughter in his ears. But Bob, according to his lights, has done his job; he has 'witnessed'.

It is embarrassing to be confronted by Bob when he has learnt a new gospel 'chorus'. Then, no matter where he happens to be, he will immediately convey what he refers to as his latest 'blessing'. This consists in giving a spirited rendering of the new chorus in a singularly harmony-proof voice. With studied deliberation, he will systematically 'murder' not only the composer's brain-child but also the self-respect of his hearer. If it happens to be on a Monday morning in the erecting shop, so much the worse. Bob always puts his flourishes and nuances to the words so they usually sound like the famous 'Grease and fever'. 'Grease and fever' expelled from the powerful lungs of Robert with a grinning galaxy of onlookers does not help the cause of Christian unity.

I once had the embarrassing experience of having Bob join me on the front seat of the top deck of a bus when I was on my way to conduct a Sunday evening service out of town. Bob is also a local preacher and he was engaged on a similar mission. When he saw me sitting there he cried 'Hallelujah!' in undisguised joy. I groaned inside when I saw that he was carrying the large hexagonal box which contained his concertina, for I knew what was about to happen. After he had wriggled himself comfortably into position beside me, he said in an animated tone of voice, "Ere, I 'ad a real blessing the other night; 'ave you 'eard this?' and having slithered his hands into the tight straps of his concertina, he flung back his head and rather like the Hound of the Baskervilles, commenced . . .

Feeling that the rest of the passengers could only see the back of my head blushing a deep crimson, I made a few unintelligible sounds in the back of my throat and nodded approvingly with the ghost of a smile – which might have been a wicked leer – hovering on my face.

One of the most colourful characters to enter the Works and certainly one of the worst adverts for Christianity was Cecil. His Elijah-like entrance into the repair shop caught everyone unawares. Cecil wore his hair Nazarite-like – white, lank and long. He had the profile of an Old Testament prophet with a splendid aquiline nose, deep-sunk eyes and a fortnight's growth of hair on his chin. With his arresting voice – undeniably sweet when he used it to sing – he momentarily exercised an authoritative hold over the men in the shop; that is, until they 'rumbled' him and discovered the chinks in his armour.

Cecil was put on the brush – sweeping the shop floor. He had once been a dustman but now, under the beneficent aegis of British Rail, he had graduated to the brush. On his first day in the shop he had flung a handful of coins on to the shop floor and shouted in his stentorian voice, 'Me 'eavenly Father provides for all me wants!' a gesture which doubtless bolstered his personal faith but caused the men to go into a series of huddles while they debated this new, and rather odd character.

Cecil soon discovered where I worked and tried to plant a 'holy kiss' on my cheek. I dissuaded him in what he considered to be a most uncharitable manner. 'But we're *brothers!*' he said disarmingly.

'*Only* brothers!' I caustically replied, 'and anyway, if you'll take my tip, you won't go around throwing your money all over the place – it sets a bad example.'

'Don't you believe that God provides?'

'Of course, but we mustn't be daft. We have hands with which to work and brains with which to think.

'Ah!' said Cecil huffily, 'I can see *you're* not "all out"!'

On the second day, he walked up to a man who was smoking and belligerently told him that 'smoking was a filthy habit' adding the old chestnut that if God had intended men to smoke he would have put chimneys on their heads. The man, with calm deliberation, took his cigarette from his lips, blew the smoke into Cecil's face and in a strange, unnatural tone said, 'Hop it – quick!'

Slowly, it began to dawn on the men that they had what they termed a 'card' on their hands and accordingly, began to make Cecil's life a misery.

They put sand in his tea.

Stuffed nuts and bolts in his pockets.

Nailed his brush to the wall.

Sewed up the sleeves and trousers of his overalls.

Hid his wheelbarrow.

Cecil bore his martyrdom with tight-lipped disapproval. He felt that these things had come to pass for what he considered was his 'straight from the shoulder, no nonsense, no compromise, hard hitting testimony.' His mates regarded the situation in a somewhat different light.

On one occasion, a very senior member of the staff, Donald Waterson, who was also a practising Christian and known to Cecil, was walking through the workshop on a tour of inspection with his colleagues – also lofty stars on the industrial firmament.

Cecil was wheeling his barrow laden with steel shavings to the dump when their paths happened to cross. 'Well, well, it is a glorious morning brother Donald, ain't it?' he pointedly enthused. 'See you at the Youth for Christ Rally next Saturday?' and as Cecil warbled on quite unselfconsciously in this palsy-walsy manner, 'Donald', poor man, put on his best charcoal-grey smile and clucked 'Quite, quite' in a mechanical way. The rest of the party stood as immobile and speechless as Nelson's Column.

We tried to temper Cecil's ardour in such matters but he seriously questioned 'Donald's' religious profession when the latter's embarrassment was pointed out. 'After all,' he said with an injured expression on his face, 'ain't we all *brothers*? – there ain't no class distinction up there!' Poor Cecil, he only reigned a short while but the few months he was with us were embarrassing and quite unpredictable!

4. All Out!

At some time in his career, the Christian must face up to the question of Union membership. After listening to the views of some of the men he may form the opinion that the Union is the workers' policeman patrolling the industrial beat and protecting the interests of the proletariat against unscrupulous bosses who would revert back to the ugly thirties at the drop of a hat. Some of the shop stewards whom he meets will undoubtedly be gifted with loud, persuasive voices and little knowledge. Others will be reasonable men with a quick grasp of the Union Rule book, a native skill in negotiation and the ability to communicate the involved arguments of the manager's office to the men on the shop floor.

Until the Industrial Relations Bill became law, the terms of reference for shop stewards were misty and undefined. They are the mouthpieces of the men, the bridge between Union and Management, the interpreters of official Union policy, the watershed of innovations on the shop floor; indeed the backbone of British industry lies in the power of its shop stewards.

If a country gets the government it deserves, the shop gets the stewards it votes into office, and it is not always the reasonable, clear-thinking candidate who secures the biggest majority. It would be a good thing if more Christians were represented in the shop steward ranks but it is hardly surprising that their numbers are so few. After all, Christianity moves on the vertical as well as the horizontal plane. The Christian is a temperate man who sees the other chap's point of view, who is quite prepared to make concessions and happily compromises when no

33

vital principles are at stake. This attitude is in striking contrast to the militancy on the shop floor for the whole *mores* of the shop are locked in a class-consciousness which sees Capital and Labour as perpetually warring factions.

Responsible Union leadership has a man-size task in damping down the bush fire disruptions on the shop floor. Unofficial strike action may sometimes spring from legitimate grievances, and combustion builds up while negotiations are taking place. Where official Union representatives see hard bargaining and patient negotiating, the men see only procrastination and bureaucracy on the part of the Management.

Again, the anarchistic attitude may develop from the fact that there is no *status* in the Union machinery. Bill Bloggs the District Secretary, Sam Slash the Shop Steward, Dan Dodge the Collector, the National President, the Executive and the General Secretary are all on an equal footing in the eyes of the men on the shop floor. They are the paid servants, therefore they must articulate the views of the men. Discipline and dictatorship are synonymous terms to many in the workshops.

The Christian, however, will discover that there are other aspects of the Union – much less publicized – which are carried on behind the scenes. Many men have cause to be grateful for the strong arm of the Union when they have sustained an injury during the course of their employment. The expensive and complicated legal procedures in claiming compensation are undergirded by the Union who provide legal representation for the claimant. The particular industry in which he is employed may also be represented in Parliament – the NUR has several MP's. Accident, death, care of orphans, retirement, unjust suspension benefits – all these come as a valuable social service to the Union member and his family.

But Trade Unions are not solely concerned with discussing the pay and conditions of the workers; in the political field they undergird the Socialist party and the Trade Union Congress represents the political arm of the unions. A Christian, or anyone else for that matter who owns to no political affiliation and who objects to paying the political levy, *can* contract out.

Whether the Christian joins a Trade Union is a matter for his individual conscience. In a large industry employing half a million workers it is manifestly impossible to conduct individual agreements respecting pay and conditions. On the other hand, there is little scope for recognizing individual qualities of good workmanship and conscientiousness when workers are dealt with *en masse*. As H. F. R. Catherwood has pointed out in his valuable book, *The Christian in Industrial Society* (Tyndale Press, 1964).

> 'The conscientious argument against joining a Union is usually based on the injunction 'Be ye not unequally yoked together with unbelievers . . . ' It is hard to reconcile this interpretation of the 'unequal yoke' with such passages as Romans 13 . . . If we are to be realistic we must certainly agree that trades unions perform a useful and necessary function. No better machinery has been found to protect the individual in our society as it is organized and potentially, at least, they are capable of much constructive work' (p.39).

My own experience with Judd might be illuminating. Judd is a shop steward and a *smart* fellow.

'You want a bag of cement – cheap?' – see Judd.

'Wood?' – see Judd.

'Ties? Socks? Shirts? Contraceptives?' – see Judd.

When Judd canvassed the shop for his election as shop steward he tried to convey the image of a Father-confessor, bring-your-troubles-to-Zilla kind of man, a compound of John Noble, Mary Brown and the Old Codgers.

I had a bad attack of Early Brethrenism at one juncture in my spiritual pilgrimage and decided to opt out of the Union.

'Conscientious grounds?' said Judd in an unbelieving tone. 'A working man can't *afford* to 'ave a conscience when it comes to securin' 'is rights.'

'I don't want to argue,' I stubbornly persisted, 'I just want to contract out of the Union.'

'You won't be popular with the boys!'

'I realize that. I don't want to be a martyr – it's just hard lines if you force me into that position.'

With a snarl in his eyes, Judd tried another tack. 'Call yourself a *Christian*, when you'll let your own mates contribute towards negotiating your rises – you'll take the rises, won'cha?' Here, he triumphantly sneered, 'Go on, hop it. When this place becomes a closed shop, you'll see where you'll be!' and with that final retort, the articulate Judd departed.

A few weeks later I was visited by Mr Bigg who was considerably further advanced than Judd on the Union ladder. 'Can I have a word with you?' he enquired pleasantly.

'Certainly,' I replied feeling highly honoured by his august presence in the mean corner where I ate my 'snap'.

'I hear you want to pull out of the Union; now, *if* that is true, tell me why.' And here his tone became conspiratorial, 'If it's as Jack Judd says – on religious grounds, don't forget the history of Trade Unions. The first Unionists were Christians – the Luddites and all that!'

'But if I remain in the Union it means that I might be compelled to take joint action and possibly act contrary to what I believe is right. And anyway, the Trade Union Movement undergirds the Socialist Party and I'm strictly non-political.'

'But you *can't* be non-political; you belong to the working class.'

'That doesn't mean I have to have political affiliations. What function do the Unions perform when a Socialist government is in power?'

'We protect the workers' interests.'

'With a workers' government in power? The very fact of having Capital and Labour in opposite camps is an admission of failure.'

'You're too fluffy with your ideas, too idealistic by far.' Mr Bigg was obviously rattled but genuinely concerned about

36

altering my ideas for my own good. 'Look here!' he went on, 'when I go into the gaffer's office to negotiate a pay rise, I see *them* on one side of the table; *they* belong to a different set-up and I'm determined to squeeze all I possibly can out of *them*.' Noticing the viciousness in his tone, I realized then why we had the threat of a strike hanging over our heads once every twelve months.

'That's a twisted way of negotiating settlements,' I replied cautiously.

'When you've been in as many wage talks as I have, you'll be able to crow but until you've had a go, I'd shut up if I was you!'

So I shut up. And withdrew my Union support.

The squeeze came gently; the moral pressure built up slowly. The conflict between the actual business of tearing up my Union card and the ideal reasons behind it became much more accentuated.

Mr Bigg saw me clocking-in every morning; he did not ignore me or look down his nose and his good-natured smile slugged my somewhat militant morality senseless.

'Can I give my Union contribution to the Widows' Benevolent Fund or the Railway Orphanage?' I asked him one day.

''Fraid not – no provision laid down in the rules and regs for siphoning Union dues into charitable concerns,' he replied unhelpfully.

The passage of time protectively wadded my sensitive conscience until the inevitable round of wage negotiations broke down. These protracted discussions usually began with the Unions asking for an absurd rise, the Management refusing it and making an equally absurd offer. This Eastern-bazaar technique usually concluded with both sides posing for the press photographers, smiling with their eyes but scowling in their hearts.

'Although this does not measure up to our just claim, we have settled for *nth* per cent in the hope that our next claim – which we shall lodge in the near future – will make up the deficit' – the Union would give its version of the outcome of the talks.

'Increased productivity is the price we must pay for higher wages, the cost of this rise will inevitably fall on the travelling public . . . ' and the BR Management would add its postmortem.

This time it was different. The play-acting did not go according to pattern. The Union said 'eight per cent – or else!' The Management, equally adamant said 'four per cent, and not a penny more!' and the crunch came: all out on strike after the statutory three weeks' notice.

When the day of the strike was announced, Pat (my wife) and I held a council of war. 'We'll pray about it first,' she said with deliberation. So we prayed and after prayer my brain clicked into a more practical gear, 'I'll draw no money at all from anywhere,' I explained bleakly, 'and if the strike goes on for any length of time . . . ' and I left the remainder unsaid.

During the next three weeks frenzied efforts took place to avert the strike; the Ministry of Labour; the TUC General Finance Committee and the TV programmers – acting as the nation's social antiseptic, all participated in the peace moves.

'As it's a privilege to suffer for Christ,' said Pat one day, 'perhaps we should welcome the opportunity of showing our colours; after all, we won't get any strike pay because you stood for what you believe is a Christian principle.'

'But I don't like the idea of you and the children paying the price of my principles!'

'They aren't only *your* principles, they're *ours* too,' she replied reassuringly.

'But the children don't understand, it doesn't seem fair to them.'

'Even the men who are paid strike money won't receive such a fat lot – two pounds ten isn't it?' asked Pat with an eye firmly fixed on the family budget.

'Better than nothing at all!'

'Oh, brighten up! We haven't any money in the bank to

38

complicate things and the Lord has promised never to leave us nor forsake us, so don't be a misery!'

'Anyway, I hope it doesn't come off,' I added gloomily.

Bert was in a similar situation to myself but without the liability of having a small family to feed. He pugnaciously suggested that we should march to the gates of the works and defiantly challenge the pickets. But we well knew that the picket lines would be manned by tough, resolute men who believed in the justice of their cause, and anyway we would not be displaying the spirit of Christ by courting violence.

Tom was naturally docile, content to sit it out. As with Bert, his only dependant was his wife.

Bob, a Methodist, took a radically different view to the rest of the Cell. He related his Christianity to his political creed – a militant Left Wing Socialism which often erupted into passionate declarations of faith in Keir Hardie rather than Christ. A slight edge of bitterness crept into his tone when he challenged me as to my dogmatic, no-strike, anti-Union attitude.

'I don't see how you can stand aside and protest that we should not come out on strike when some of the lower-paid blokes are taking home less than eleven quid a week!' he heatedly reminded me. 'Can you picture Paul or John or Peter condoning such social injustices?'

'Can you imagine Peter a rip-roaring Tory or Paul a fire-eating Communist or John a passionate Socialist?' I replied. 'Christ said, "I am not of this world"; Paul said "Be not unequally yoked with unbelievers"; Peter said "Save yourselves from this crooked generation"; John said "Love not the world neither the things that are in the world". How does your view of life square with the Scriptures?' Bob snorted in disgust and shook his head in a gesture of hopeless frustration and stalked off.

Opinion on the shop floor was sharply divided. The older men with long memories of 1926 cautioned against strike action – 'there's now't ever been gained through a strike' was their general reaction; but the younger element, always anxious to show their dads what pussyfeet they'd been in '26, advocated an all out fight to a victorious finish.

During the week preceding the stoppage deadline a note of cynicism was detected in the canteen debates. The news broke that the Minister for Economic Affairs had lit the flares for the Prime Minister to home-in on the proceedings. As zero hour approached the tension was heightened to an almost unbearable level.

With less than twenty-four hours to go, Pat and I said our prayers before turning in. 'Do you think it will come off?' yawned Pat.

'If it does, we'll just have enough to pay the rent!' I croaked.

While we were asleep, the lights in 10 Downing Street burned long into the night, and over beer and sandwiches – which may have been a late supper or an early breakfast – agreement was reached without loss of face to either side.

'Are *you* going to have the nerve to take the rise?' asked Bob next day. The heavily accentuated 'you' hit me hard in my spiritual solar plexus with its implications of a fractured friendship.

'Look here, Bob, we musn't allow these things to interfere with our essential relationship. We *are* Christians!' I answered.

'That's the very point I'm trying to make – you have an obligation to your neighbour!'

'But it's moral blackmail to expect me to toe the Union line before you accept my attitude as being "Christian".'

I arrived home that night disconsolate and argument-weary. Pat was sympathetic. 'Have an early night,' she advised, 'I'll bring you a cup of Ovaltine and you can sleep it off.'

'I can't sleep off moral issues. Bob's right in one way. You can't put your conscience to sleep and hope it will wake fresh and uncomplicated in the morning.'

'Are you *sure* it's your conscience? Maybe it's a misplaced loyalty or perhaps a line of argument that is loaded . . . !' and

Pat's final curtain on all-things-difficult-to-resolve was announced. 'We'll pray about it . . . ' she said cheerfully.

A week later I went to Mr Bigg and with an affirmative nodding of the head and sympathetic grunts he listened to what I had to say: ' . . . and so you see Mr Bigg, although I disagree with many aspects of Union policy I realize that I put myself in an invidious position by not contributing to the Union; I have a social responsibility and I'll contribute to the Union but take no active part in its affairs!'

Judd threw a sneer in my direction, 'I knew you'd *'ave* to see sense!' he said.

Mr Bigg genially beamed.

Bob was affable, the wandering sheep had returned to the fold and all was forgiven.

Pat was relieved of another item on her prayer list and I looked at my Brethren books in the bookcase with their stout backings, their cryptic author-initials and distinctive phraseology and I hung my head, perhaps in shame or maybe in perplexity.

5. A Question of Colour

With an influx of coloured people into Moortown, it was tacitly understood that the Works Committee were unitedly opposed to coloured labour; a quiet but effective colour bar was exercised, until from the higher echelons of power pressure was exerted on the Committee and the first trickle of Commonwealth immigrants took their places on the shop floor.

The day was typically dreary when they arrived; outside the gaunt and ugly Victorian workshops, with their cornices and arches exuding their own mournful antiquity, were silhouetted against a weeping sky. Within the shops the unbelievable confusion of ironmongery, grease and din somehow added up to Pullman coaches.

The Jamaicans and Indians stood in a group outside the shop office looking completely dejected and woebegone, their wide brown eyes mirroring the ugliness and chaos of the British industrial scene. One odd-looking character was wearing an army greatcoat obviously two sizes too large and his frizzy hair protruded from beneath the curious Stetson hat he wore . . . they were a long memory away from the sun-drenched beaches of Tobago Bay.

Another wretched-looking fellow stood shivering in a hat rather similar to the Chinese army pattern, the muffs of which flapped around his ears as the bitter east wind whistled through the cracks in the big double doors of the shop.

They silently regarded their place of employment while their various jobs were being sorted out in the office. Meanwhile, a hot debate was taking place in No. 2 Bay.

'The cats'll welcome 'em. These coves eat Kit-e-kat sandwiches and they buy lights and stuff from the Pets' meat shop and make stew of it!' This information was volunteered by ignorant hatchet-faced Eddie, a learned character in such matters as Littlewood's pools and Nemo's tickets but hardly qualified to pass an opinion or volunteer information on such matters as race relations.

'They're funny tempered wallahs' said Steve in a menacing tone. 'Carry knives too!'

'They smell of garlic.'

'They've got queer ideas about women.'

'They have parties that last all night and *hundreds* go!'

'They're dirty and diseased.'

'They get an easy touch at the NA.'

And so on . . .

What lay behind this attitude? The opposition encountered by the coloured folk in Moortown was, perhaps understandably, a compound of ignorance and fear. Thirty years ago we were still being taught that the 'blacks' were an inferior race. 'The black man will get you!' 'Your mother's run off with a black man!' 'A blackie will gobble you up if you are naughty' – these were the salutary warnings at the time of what might happen if we youngsters did not toe the parental line, and inevitably there may be subconsciously a lingering deposit of suspicion for anyone with a differently coloured skin.

Perhaps more real is the fear that too much coloured labour in the country will create greater social problems than the mere irritation of all-night parties and the chocolate-coloured barrier propping up Woolworth's refreshment counter on Saturday afternoons. In a time of economic 'cooling off' an expanded labour force and a choosey management may well produce a situation both alien and repulsive to the British way of life. Hungry men do not pause to consider abstract moral questions; when jobs are scarce they are more likely to claim that the country of their birth owes *them* a living rather than the immigrant.

In many cases they have been housed in the run-down areas,

in districts which used to be fashionable residential areas where local notables lived – the doctor, the solicitor and the business man. But their former elegance has disappeared. Now, the immigrants have bought the large houses, some of which have been converted into flats and others communally shared. In these overcrowded areas gardens are often neglected and some become repositories for scooters, dustbins and children's toys.

To the British the ways of foreigners may seem strange. Some find it hard to see tradition breaking down: as Pakistani and Indian women clad in gaily coloured saris and silk trousers make their way to the supermarket; as small grocery shops, now owned by immigrants, have erected exotic signs extolling even more exotic foods and the familiar Reckitt's Blue or Persil notices have gone.

The immigrants did not blend easily into the rather grubby background of Moortown life; they monopolized the refreshment counter in the local Woolworths on a Saturday afternoon and talked in high falsetto voices as they counted their change. In public parks they grouped together and formed card-schools while the locals looked on, their insularity acting as a heat shield between what they really felt and the coloured people.

In the interests of the public the local press indignantly demanded a curb on the immigration quota and a thoroughgoing medical check-up on those who had recently arrived. This inky indignation was answered by 'Myrtle Moonshine' who, with equal passion, advanced the view that as we were 'the Mother of the Commonwealth' these people had an inalienable *right* to come, and anyway what about the Southern Irish, the Hungarians and Poles? And the exchanges went on until the editor felt that readers' letters on race relations were hogging all the space to the detriment of those concerned about more mundane affairs like late buses and dogs fouling the pavements of Moortown.

Words like 'integration' 'multi-racial' 'segregation' are now accepted as part of the vocabulary of the well-informed on the shop floor. In discussions among the men, the usual conclusion is that 'the end place of integration is the bedroom'.

Yet one seriously wonders whether, say, the Sikh with his ancient cultural heritage wants to be integrated, and certainly the last thing the men on the shop floor desire is to be reduced into the grey – or coffee coloured – uniformity so dearly envisaged by the starry-eyed social engineers of the various political parties.

There appears to be a distinct difference in the attitude and outlook of various national groups. On the one hand, some of the Indians and Pakistanis seem to be content to be withdrawn and isolated from European Society. They retain many of their habits and social customs of their homelands and display no undue anxiety to conform to the British way of life. 'East is East and West is West' is a truism which neither they nor we show any signs of desiring to contest.

The West Indians, for the most part, are an extrovert community. Their boisterous good humour and infectious gaiety spill over into every aspect of their lives; their songs are rhythmic and simple; their temperaments volatile and keenly sensitive to discrimination.

I must confess that the coming of the coloured workers awoke in me a latent resentment which I found most difficult to rationalize. Was it merely colour? A clash of cultures? A colour bar that was quite naturally sired by differences too deep to be ignored? A subconscious reaction that they were strangers with different pigmentation and therefore a different nature?

As a Christian I realized that these questions were completely inadmissible for, on the human level, Jesus had a semitic background. He asked a favour of a Samaritan woman who was living in sin, commended the faith of a Roman centurion, communicated His gospel to the Gentiles through a Roman Jew and sent His emissary to an Ethiopian eunuch. My natural instincts had violated a Christian principle, which I had hitherto felt was completely inviolable.

One Sunday at the small church where I worshipped, a little, ebony-coloured man quietly seated himself beside me. We exchanged smiles and his was a flashing 'Macleaner' that almost lit the room. His suit was well-cut and his finger nails perfectly manicured, his Bible well-thumbed and he sat composedly waiting for the service to begin. Other folk in the congregation gave him faintly patronizing smiles – rather tight-lipped and mechanical. However, this had nothing to do with his colour. He was a stranger in our midst and his nationality was sub-servient to the main consideration of making him feel at home, so Thomas was introduced to the church.

He quickly identified himself with the congregation and, after a few weeks, was regarded with the same affection and understanding as anyone else. My awareness regarding the 'colour problem' began about this time. With Thomas' active participation in the 'free' type of worship to which we at the church are accustomed, other West Indians were also attracted. We soon discovered that they thought we were rather sterile in our approach to worship, that the reality of God was not so apparent as in the type of meeting to which they were accus-tomed back home. Their animated 'Amen's!' and spontaneous 'Hallelujahs!' as they expressed total agreement with the preacher's remarks were rather overpowering and they livened up the tempo of the hymns in a spectacular way. However, their exuberant sincerity was an irritant which even the most tolerant and charitable found it hard to ignore. After a time, with mutual expressions of goodwill, they left to form their own indigenous congregation. Thomas, quite surprisingly, seemed more attuned to our more staid and prosaic approach to worship and he decided to stay with us.

He had a phenomenal memory for the verses of hymns. When he prayed extempore it was as though he had opened 'Hymns Ancient and Modern!' With arms extended and eyes tightly closed and a pacific calm on his face he would begin:

Now thank we all our God,
With hearts and hands and voices . . .
O wisest love! that flesh and blood
Which did in Adam fail, . . .
Thy right would we give Thee (and)
We worship and adore Thee
Before the mercy seat . . .

and so on.

Thomas was a navvy, but a more unlikely navvy you could not wish to meet. His demeanour and polished manners were quite out of character with the nature of his work. He was a most gracious man and displayed all the shining attributes of the Christian character.

Through him I was introduced to a wider variety of his compatriots and I was able to clarify my earlier, superficial views. While they were different in their background and culture, their aspirations as Christians were precisely the same as my own; Calvary is the common denominator. But there could be no question of integration in the sense of both nationalities being submerged into a common whole.

The professional politician with one eye on the coloured vote and the other on some 'progressive' obscure ideological issue may pontificate about 'colour prejudice' and 'fascist conspiracy'; but he is out of touch with reality. Here in Moortown, the churches have shown the way and extended a practical hand of friendship to the coloured community with the result that there is now a thriving West Indian Community centre. Here, against a Christian background, the Thomases and their wives may meet their compatriots and together, with the locals, experience new dimensions of fellowship.

One local parish church regularly holds a 'Caribbean Evening' when the two communities – English and West Indian – meet together and in an atmosphere of mutual goodwill 'good-neighbourliness' is allowed to flourish naturally.

As Christians we have a built-in resolve not to be influenced

47

by any colour prejudice but there is no doubt that the banter of some of the men on the shop floor directed towards the coloured immigrants might turn the hair of members of the local Race Relations Board grey overnight! Often the men are not being vicious or prejudiced but are simply displaying their bent sense of humour. Perhaps Larry, the West Indian who was asked if lions wandered around his home village and whether he carried a spear back home, might secretly have wished he had a pet lion and a handy spear in the workshop. And the courteous West African who took a job as a labourer while waiting to enter University and was nicknamed 'The Cannibal' by the rest of the gang, although he showed no apparent resentment, must surely have formed his own views about the men with whom he was working.

Those with whom we work will notice our attitude to the coloured minority. To be distanced from other men because of difference of colour reveals a serious defect in our relationship to Christ. If prejudice is present in our make-up a spiritual overhaul is required to examine and trace the causes. The Christian is a realist: to recognize the hair-cracks which appear in the earthen vessels carrying the gospel-treasure is a sign of maturity. The sin lies in neglecting to do anything about the matter once it has been brought to light. Our thoughtlife must be guarded and the 'mind of Christ' eagerly pursued and cultivated; we must beware of the subtle erosion of our values that may occur unconsciously as we listen to the specious and persuasive arguments of some of the men when they dilate on 'Black Power' and the threat to the white man's job.

The Church has a leading role to play in building up a harmonious relationship between the various racial groups. In industry, where the thin veneer of High Street respectability cushioning the clash of creeds and colours has been removed, the Christian has an important task to fulfil.

6.   Out on the Fringe

The kind of men a Christian in industry rubs shoulders with are, for the most part, individuals who live tidy lives of strict conformity. Their behaviour patterns are predictable and one may safely gauge, say, popular opinion on a National Lottery, or the jaundiced reception H. F. R. Catherwood's remark might get when he writes:

> 'The men in No. 2 Bay may not see why they should change working habits because the young work study engineer has come up with some bright idea for doubling the output. But when, eventually, an incentive scheme is worked out and No. 1 Bay are taking home £4 a week more, the majority in No. 2 Bay will probably decide to give the scheme a try and before long the old way of work will seem rather stupid to them.' *

The fact is that the men will probably want to know who gets the sack so that the rest can have £4 a week extra.

Their domestic lives are not all *Saturday Night and Sunday Morning* and their daughters are not all *Up the Junction* misfits; there are few Alf Garnets and Andy Capps among them. These larger-than-life caricatures bear little resemblance to the actual figures. For the Christian the 'Man on the Clapham Omnibus' must remain a shadowy legal convenience, unrelated to the distinctive personalities of the Jack Smiths, Bill Robinsons and Harry Browns. It is a melancholy fact that most of my workmates live in architecturally flat and featureless

* *The Christian in Industrial Society*, p. 24

council houses that are strictly utilitarian – 'Planned for Plain People' – and the monotonous regularity of design in both environment and pattern of living leads to a dreary standardization.

In all large groupings however, there will inevitably be individuals who cannot be categorized. Some are rejects of society, oddities who are more pathetic than humorous in their appeal. Others are highly articulate men who have cut a clearing of eccentric belief in a forest of orthodoxy. These characters live out their lives on the fringe of our ordered society in the workshops.

The whole spectrum of political and religious conviction is covered in the works. The Welsh navvy who critically reads the *New Statesman* and *The Guardian*; the Irish labourer who is a devout Roman Catholic and studies Greek with dogged determination; 'Red Ted', the Communist who voluntarily surrenders his leisure time to sell the *Morning Star* outside the main gate before he joins his mates to clock on for the early morning shift; the Rosicrucian who zealously pursues his particular line . . .

There is a gradual shading-off between the committed Christian and the majority of the workers who have no religious interest whatsoever. In this overlap there are the nominal Christians who, together with their wives, go to church every Sunday evening, and for these the church is a social convenience slotted into their workaday lives as an insurance policy against Acts of God and the follies of man. They prefer a 'sacred concert' type of service with a short sermonette, a few 'good old Sankey hymns' and a 'comforting prayer'. If the Police Choir is there to give a spirited rendering of *The Lost Chord*, so much the better. The fact that they put ten pence in the collection plate is an added source of comforting assurance.

The notion that Christianity demands an ethical response is entirely removed from their thinking; they have *made* that response, they have *been* to church, they have *given* their alms,

50

what more can possibly be required? The fact that they tell dirty stories and do all manner of things inside the works that they would not dream of doing outside is entirely irrelevant and easily explained: they don't *mean* what they say, and after all one may easily be branded 'fanatical' or slightly 'tapped' if one rises on one's spiritual hackles and strikes an attitude of nonconformity in what is predominantly a conformist society.

The Roman Catholics have their own brand of logic to justify their weekday attitudes and activities as opposed to their ritualistic Sabbath worship. The general impression among the uncommitted workers is that, for the RC's at any rate, this strange dichotomy is permissible. Perhaps the ingrained respect of the Englishman for history and tradition is responsible for this conciliatory attitude toward the Roman Catholics. Certainly, the Irish labourer never hides his particular denominational light under a bushel of apologies but proclaims with due reverence his identity with the Holy Mother Church, and will inform any interested enquirer that as a matter of religious duty he has been to Mass at 7 a.m. on a wet Wednesday morning in January prior to starting work. The industrial leadership courses at Loyola Hall, the Jesuit Community in Liverpool, and its aim of forming '100 per cent Christian dockers, miners . . . trade unionists' may be as remote as the dodo from the Irish labourer but he is nonetheless devoted to his faith and may have tremendous regard for his priest.

Then there are those who are affiliated to the fringe sects and hold strange and heterodox views which effectively insulate them from all other factions. Invariably, when a Jehovah's Witness, Christadelphian, or Rosicrucian is manoeuvered into a position where he must stand to be counted, he is able to argue cogently and convincingly. Usually, the man who belongs to a fringe sect is a model worker, owns to a high moral code and has a vocational sense of responsibility even when engaged in the most boring and menial tasks. He is courteous and patient when stating his doctrine – particularly when he is engaged in a verbal tussle with an interested and genuine enquirer. The

Christian who is unsure of his doctrine would be wise to refrain from being drawn into controversy with the well-drilled member of a heterodox sect. Any argument or discussion on the shop floor draws an interested circle of onlookers; they are very partisan and come down heavily on the side of the skilled debater.

I have never met a believer in the Flat Earth theory nor have I had the experience of meeting a 'Cornwall for the Cornish' enthusiast. But I have met Slab.

Slab was a diminutive man with a cadaverous, bony face and a sallow complexion. His large watery-blue eyes had a perpetual far away look, for Slab was a mystic of the first order. Meeting him for the first time was a slightly unnerving experience for then he told me he had been gambolling on the astral plane the previous evening and held social intercourse with Ancient Romans. I recall the strange compound of curiosity and bewilderment I felt as I eyed him standing there with his pushcart laden with cotton waste, telling me of his strange adventures. Not content with pursuing mind-bending exercises such as staring at his navel in his meditative sessions, he subscribed to the Rosicrucian fraternity. He flatly refused to describe or divulge their esoteric beliefs but explained that the local group met regularly in the remote hills near Moortown at some secluded spot safe from prying eyes.

One day in an unguarded moment he did liberate some of his closely guarded secrets and explained that each morning, two golden tablets appeared before him on waking and they were inscribed with precepts he must carry out on that day. Needless to say, I was most intrigued by this revelation and decided to cultivate our friendship still further.

I discovered that Slab had no other hobbies except reading obscure Indian poets and studying Rosicrucian literature. His wife was understandably distanced from him: ' 'E were never like it afore,' she explained; 'when we got married 'e were normal, like, but 'e got funny, kind of, over the years, sort of . . . '

Slab's teenage daughter Marjorie was a wan-faced young lady who struck up an amorous partnership with a married man, and Slab's wife with an adamant look in her eye remarked emphatically, 'She's 'avin' 'er baby at 'ome: *I* wouldn't 'ave it any other way.'

Slab viewed his domestic life with a philosophical eye, an Anglo-Saxon brand of Eastern fatalism washing away the realities of a frustrated wife and a promiscuous daughter.

He believed that Jesus Christ was a Rosicrucian and that He travelled to India; he also advanced the theory that the *true* Bible is somehow to be identified with secret manuscripts in a remote Tibetan monastery and these can only be deciphered by the Rosicrucians. These views automatically categorized him as a harmless eccentric, or perhaps, an amiable fanatic. But like all Men with a Message, Slab had his tight little coterie of willing listeners during snap time. Flying Saucers, the Pyramids of Giza, the Mystery of Stonehenge, Mythical Atlantis, the Devil's Hoofprints . . . a fascinating array of fact, fable, fiction and fantasy was trundled into view, exposed and explained before the mystified and admiring eyes of Slab's followers. Their jaws sagged in undisguised awe as he propounded his theories of the Universe and unfolded Nature's Secrets Hidden Since Time Began.

Slab's chief disciple was Ernie Blunt. Ernie was sufficiently innoculated with a soporific brand of churchianity to ensure that virile Christianity was warded off. His church boasted a new extension incorporating a Community Hall, luxuriously furnished and fully licensed, a coffee bar, a cinema annexe and other expensive trimmings. Ernie was a leading figure in the affairs of this place. As the Sunday School Superintendent he certainly looked the part; twinkling eyes that were always laughing, a roly-poly figure and puckish mouth – the children loved him.

True, he did not believe in hell and his theology was fractured in the evangelical sense but he was a rare 'do-gooder' and Slab's hypnotic speech hooked him. Ernie did not allow his bottom jaw to sag like the rest nor were his eyes glazed with credulous wonder as Slab expounded his themes. He sat with his chin cupped in the palm of his hands as he squinted his eyes in wrapt concentration. Soon he was deeply involved in Slab's off-beat fraternity. It may not have been the doctrine of the American headquarters of the Rosicrucian Order – maybe it was the fanciful interpretations of the local branch – but whatever it was the teaching took a lethal swipe at Ernie's tenuous hold on orthodox Christian doctrine and he was sold, lock stock and barrel on Slab's view on life.

A strange compound of Rosicrucianism, Christian Science, Jehovah's Witness teaching and general hobgoblinism now took precedence over the staid and colourless brand of religion Ernie had half-heartedly practised. The conversation of Slab and Ernie now assumed a somewhat surrealist flavour as they enthused about their astral plane wanderings and the special kind of mental gymnastics in which they indulged each morning. We tried to wean Ernie away from Slab during the early stages of this bizarre soul-mating but alas we failed. Perhaps Slab was the soul-mate he was supposed to meet anyway. At least Slab thinks this is possible; they are looking forward to teaming up in a reincarnated sense, having progressed up the ladder of life, so to speak.

But the salutary truth rises to the surface in this particular pool of qualified humour: Ernie has 'seen the light' and Slab's half-baked ideas are floating round in his eight ounces of pulsating jellied mass. He is free and eager to propagate his ideas as a flaming evangelist of mumbo-jumboism. One hesitates to think of the choruses the Sunday School children may be taught to sing should some Indian spirit-guide lead Ernie to be the emanuensis of some Druidic bard. Ernie has been a pillar of the Church for forty years but in the light of his relationship with Slab the pillar needs a good deal of healthy support.

Such men as Slab and Ernie are a liability to the practising Christian because the rest of the men are inclined to regard every man who mentions the name of Christ in a serious vein as an orthodox believer. Having had only a scanty background of religious instruction they are unable to differentiate between the Jehovah's Witness interpretation of Calvary and the orthodox evangelical viewpoint and this makes communication of the gospel very difficult. The Church is institutionalized in the minds of the men; a *middle class institution* and therefore almost totally remote. Its dogmas and doctrines, forms and ceremonies, are either incomprehensible or simply rejected because of the lack of convincing evidence. Any contribution therefore which presents the truth in a more understandable and attractive fashion – even if it is 'off beat' – is always sure of a sympathetic response, and the 'fringe men' provide that contribution. It must be confessed that to some extent the evangelical Christian is a 'fringe man' to many of his workmates but does not command the same degree of 'neutral' goodwill as that meted out to the characters under review. Perhaps he is regarded as a more dangerous symbol of the Establishment, a curious anachronism elbowing its way into the industrial arena from which it should have been excluded years ago along with the rest of the social refuse – the Means Test and soup kitchen outlook on life.

Of a different order is Abby the Anarchist. Abby is fiftyish and confesses that his wife gets on his nerves, 'She's one of these wenches who have the "wants" – she wants a new 'at, she wants a new frock . . . I know what she'll *get* one of these days!' he says darkly. He sits in the corner where he hangs his coat and eats his snap. Here he holds his daily 'views on the news'. Abby is the poor man's Malcolm Muggeridge. His acid wit and provocative manner, his wry grimaces and dry humour make for an entertaining half hour. When Abby makes his negative comments on current affairs, ordinary words change their meanings and take on other forms as every shade of meaning is explored to give them new life. His faithful disciples gather to hear the master expound on the chicanery of political leaders, the hypocrisy of priestcraft and the exploitation of the working class by industrialists.

'Political tags are meaningless,' he says as he prods his briar with a match to clean out the shreds of tobacco, 'soon, only your dads will be pointin' out the difference between Toryism and Socialism – these words are meaningless and irrelevant. Anyway, the Union takes care of our interests,' he continues in a sarcastic vein, 'so why should we worry? What do we pay our two bob a week for? To sit in a hired room at the Mechanics' Institute debating whether Joe Bloggs' arm injury which he got on the lathe is worth following up? Talk about apathy in the churches! Snobby Walker – he's chairman of 6 Branch – says he has 1,700 blokes on his books and only 27 turn up every month at the Branch meeting!

'And then look what it says here,' – and he stabs his finger into the centre page of the *Daily Telegraph*. 'It says, "Trade Union membership reached a record level of 10,180,000 last year, an increase of 101,000 over 1964". Who's kidding who?' He puffs furiously at his pipe as he lights the fourth match, 'I tell you, we're being sold up the river by the depth-probe boys; we can't tell marge from butter; we prefer mints with holes in them; our fags are as cool as a mountain stream; and we brush our teeth best with *electric* toothbrushes . . . I tell you, *they* think *we're* daft.'

Abby's brain now clicks into another gear, 'We've got our telly and bingo and then these Jovial Witnesses come on the door and promise us pie in the sky when we've got strawberries and cream down here. We're the new privileged class, you see, Society takes *us* as its yardstick – that's why the Beatles get into the Honours List, Adam Faith chats it up with the Archbishop of Canterbury, Harold Wilson stands posing with the Coronation Street crew and Northern dramatists make a packet out of depicting out attitudes and responses . . .'

Abby is a great entertainer and no one takes him seriously. He is regularly seen in the Public Library on Saturday afternoons hunting down his favourites – C. E. M. Joad, George

Orwell and H. G. Wells.

Abby's defence mechanism is automatically switched on when he is challenged on spiritual matters and then the whole gamut of changing emotions can be seen – humour, ridicule, impatience, animosity. One discovers that the rather loose façade of good natured cynicism which he habitually shows to the world is not Abby's true self, but he is the living embodiment of Thoreau's observation that 'most men live lives of quiet desperation'.

Abby was one of four seamen rescued from a destroyer which went down with all hands in 1943 and only once – when he was probed about this harrowing memory – was the sprinkler system of ice-cold scorn towards evangelical Christianity held in check. On that occasion he spoke tenderly and factually about a man's relationship with his Maker; even so it was more a soliloquy and I was a sympathetic listener.

There are others who come into the fringe category. Odd men who, like wandering stars, career along a trackless path from one off-beat belief to another. The man who has held an engaging conversation with beings who arrived by Flying Saucer from a distant planet; this meeting allegedly took place in a Welsh village. The man who had a fixation about the Tennessee Valley Authority project in North America – he could not sustain a conversation for five minutes without idealizing TVA. The bibliophile who collects books with almost maniacal fervency and stores them tier upon tier in the top attic of his house – they are all here and we who are Christians sometimes feel like 'missionaries who stayed at home'. The ministry of the listening ear and open heart is still the key which unlocks many problems in the workshop and we wait praying and hoping that the next time Abby drops his guard he'll be a receptive target for what we have to say.

7. Snap

One does not need to spend a great deal of time on the workshop floor, to note how easy it is to idealize the workshop bench from the pulpit. Telling the industrial worker on Sunday that he must try and glorify God in his work is often a hopeless cliché when put to the test on Monday. One cannot hope to glorify God when, say, one is a member of a labouring gang which has been given the whole afternoon shift to perform a thirty minute job. Again, some restrictive practices, which the Christian with a corporate responsibility finds it difficult to avoid, have their origin not in the laboured debates of the Trade Union but rather in the natural man's reluctance to conform to schedules imposed by his superiors. This certainly acts as a brake on the aspiring Christian. It is easy to insist that the Christian is a separate entity and owns to a different scale of values and therefore should be the pacemaker in moral rectitude, but in practice this does not work out. He simply cannot 'go it alone' when he is a member of a labouring gang. The Christian may well be prepared to be called 'pi' in more indelicate language by his workmates without the least thought of wishing to cultivate a martyr image, but three hundredweight of metal buffer which requires manhandling into position is a constant reminder that no man is an island, and the Christian's outlook in these matters is essentially pragmatic.

If the rest of the gang feel inclined to participate in the football international at Wembley via the transistor radio while having a smoke, then our hypothetical Christian who, if for no other reason, is simply not interested in football, merely sits it out until their interest wanes or the gaffer appears.

Very often, they decide to debate the leader in the *Daily Mirror* ('Ted Goes Off Course') and the Christian is invited to comment. The conversations usually result in a stalemate: 'Hey Vic' (short for the nickname 'Vicar') 'it says 'ere that the church 'ain't wiv it – what do you say to that?'

'With what?'

'Wot it sez 'ere, "The church 'ain't wiv it".'

'What's "it"?'

'It's "it" – you know, *it*!'

But the men barely budge from their prepared intellectual bunkers. Lord Rothermere's observation that he 'bought woodpulp, processed it and sold it at a profit' may have more than a germ of truth in it for the popular newspapers with their acute sensitivity to the mass mind tailor their product accordingly. The headlines are brash and the newspaper identifies itself with the reader with just an undertone of mental superiority ('*we* say . . . '). Occasionally it takes the place of the reader and barges into the stately homes of England and bawls 'Come off it Duke!' In short, it identifies itself with the overall brigade and articulates the working man's likes and dislikes, his hopes and fears, his preferences and discriminations, for they are all there, large as life and sometimes larger: the salacious pin-ups and provocative language, the Jack Moron type of journalism, ensure an enthusiastic response from the shop floor.

To 'knock' the Establishment and be on matey terms with nobility and even have the effrontery to rap the House of Windsor is all calculated to serve the one great aim – to establish and maintain a (lucrative) rapport between the reader and his newspaper champion.

The labouring gang has a built-in aggressiveness. Many of the men served in the War and perhaps something of their military training has left a deposit. The old adage that 'a grumbling soldier is a happy soldier' certainly holds good in their case, for these fellows must have something or someone on which to vent their spleen. A dogmatic assertion that Left Foot Len should be dropped from the home team's First Eleven on Saturday might spark off a full scale row, when insulting four, five and six letter words are exchanged on a reciprocal basis. After the fury of the first few minutes, when the wrath has spent itself, the atmosphere is understandably frigid and only the steady champing of sandwiches and thirsty gulps of tea break the sullen silence. But the animosity evaporates rapidly when the chargehand makes his appearance and calls them back on the job.

These men look for inefficiency in management and are quick to make capital out of a mistaken decision or an ambiguous declaration. They exploit weakness and are suspicious of friendly overtures from the management. A cardinal sin in their eyes – much worse than a *mistaken* decision – is the inability of management to make *any* decision and they are quick to exploit this deficiency. However, they are ready to respond to capable and understanding leadership.

To argue about politics on the shop floor is as compulsive and monotonous as eating peanuts, and naturally Socialism has cradled the hopes and aspirations of the railmen through succeeding generations. The apparent *volte-face* of the Labour administration during a time of economic freeze caused a few anxious frowns on the faces of the old guard – the shop stewards and local councillors, the voluntary workers and hard core union diehards – but their fidelity never faltered and their loyalty to the Party never wavered. The arguments were always bracketed in the context of 'Them' and 'Us'. 'Them' in power is a tragedy beyond argument. Working class solidarity has been built up by outside pressures and we are never allowed to forget that our present standard of living has been gained only by the sacrificial labours of a past generation. Especially during a General Election build-up when the major parties are hankering after votes we are reminded that the working class has been thrown together by economic pressures and Capitalist policies, and now it is bonded together by organized labour in the Trades Unions and the Labour Party.

The political consciousness of the men on the shop floor is not highly developed and is understandably based on tradition and emotional reaction rather than on clearly defined principles. Jimmy Thomas, the railmen's MP in the thirties, still retains a place of affection in the hearts of the older hands. Nye Bevan, Ernie Bevin, Willie Gallacher – these were the 'greats'. The University Socialists (as distinct from working class 'Labour') with their polished and erudite explanations of Socialist philosophy are viewed with suspicion. MPs who protest the workers' cause in refined BBC accents and no dropped aspirates are viewed with suspicion; the Yorkshire burr in Mr Wilson's speech is a positive asset.

Minor irritations assume a totally unreal significance on sunny afternoons when the air is heavy with smoke and the din of the rivet guns unceasingly beats a metallic tattoo on one's ear drums. Indignation is selective – a carelessly handled bar of iron, a look of frustrated annoyance on the face of the charge-hand, a trailer loaded with bolts which refuses to be manhandled into position, or, worse, a trailer which has been turned at too sharp an angle and toppled over spilling its heavy load on to the ground. These are mishaps to be endlessly debated and argued over. Like a dog worrying a bone, these men will gnaw an imagined grievance with vehemence until knocking-off time.

The journalistic ordure of the Sunday scandal sheet forms part of the mire through which the Christian must occasionally wallow on Monday mornings. Clerics and choirmasters who figure in unsavoury court cases become symbols of a discredited institution – the Church – and every report of skullduggery in the Church is eagerly seized upon. Over the next twelve months, for every Schweitzer and Huddleston, who are forgotten anyway, there will be a dozen unfortunates who will figure prominently in the tea-break discussions. One cannot use the language of Zion on the shop floor explaining how and why men – even those who have a vocation in the Church – fall

61

into sin. My workmates do not understand that language and even if they did they would never accept the reasons advanced as to why these things happen *in the Church*. When confronted by half a dozen men gleefully brandishing an unsavoury news report it is good to preserve a sense of humour. Indeed, in any debate on the floor, humour is an indispensable part of the Christian's armoury. When one is subjected to verbal sparring and the close clinches of snide remarks, it is fatal to stand on one's dignity and try and maintain an attitude of stiff-lipped respectability. To compromise when one's temperament and susceptibilities are at stake but remain unshakeable where convictions and principles are concerned must form part of the tactics of the Christian in the workshop.

In spite of work study and streamlined production methods the tea-break is jealously guarded, and this may well represent a valuable safety valve for society! In recent years the volatile Latin, the stolid, industrial Teuton, the mercurial Frenchman and phlegmatic Russian have all had their share of internal strife – revolution, anarchy, political instability. On the other hand, except for a few minor tremors on the face of the body politic, Britain has been free from such social earthquakes.

The plot of ground where on an upturned box the mashing-can rests, is a kind of sacred fane. The mashing is strong and deep, rusty-brown in colour, and the generous spoonfuls of tea make it a nectar fit for the gods. The men sit in a circle like votaries sipping the brew and reading the newspapers, mumbling their comments and methodically demolishing the wedges of bread and dripping, meat-paste, cheese and onion, or whatever the missus has prepared. After the food comes the forum when topics of the day are debated. Sometimes these are explosive but the heat is taken out by the gaffer strategically popping up from nowhere and reminding them 'time to start, lads'. They go back to the job satisfied that the world has been righted and their opponents bested during the tea break. And mañana takes care of the rest.

Some men are very sensitive about their intellectual defects and it is prudent to allow the *faux pas* to pass unnoticed. The fellow who speaks knowledgeably to a group of serious listeners about the 'insensitive bonus' will not look too kindly on the chap who tells him his slip is showing and that the word is 'incentive'!

The young apprentice may well be regarded as an outsider whose incubation period has not yet finished, whose salary-earning maturity has yet to come, and this coupled with the fact that he is a practising Christian is a weighty cross he carries around with him. Even those who have been Christians for years experience considerable difficulty in maintaining Christian standards in the workshop when the edges of what is and what is not permissible become blurred in the mists of a permissive society. A raffle ticket for St Agatha's Blind School may be a subject of academic debate at the Young Men's Fellowship but when a flinty eyed character comes to you in the workshop clutching a bundle of tickets, one cannot pontificate on the rights and wrongs of gambling; one pays one's sixpence and declines the ticket. And if the flinty eyed character decides to keep the ticket for himself and it wins you may have lost twenty-five pounds but gained a friend – of sorts – who thinks, perhaps, you are a little odd.

The false reasoning on the shop floor may offend the conscience of some folk but this sophistry is double-edged, and what the *Daily Mirror* refers to as 'restrictive practices' the man on the shop floor sees as legitimate safeguards for the traditional rights and privileges that go with the job. The blinkered eyes of the newspaper's industrial reporter may regard the 'Go slow' as an unjustified action crippling the travelling public but the men see it as a withdrawal of goodwill, a work-to-rule, a conscientious honouring of the safety regulations. Redundancy in Whitehall is 'the sack' in Moortown and the man who disregards the call of the Union to withdraw his labour may be seen by the *Sun* as a hero of our times, but to the men he is a scab, a blackleg, a traitor who has let his mates down.

The workshop is a jungle land of rights and wrongs with a tangled undergrowth of twisted logic and the Christian must seek to exhibit those characteristics to which Paul refers in 2 Corinthians 6:

> 'As God's servants, we try to recommend ourselves by... the innocence of our behaviour, our grasp of truth, our patience and kindliness; by gifts of the Holy Spirit, by sincere love, by declaring the truth, by the power of God. We wield the weapons of righteousness in the right hand and left. Honour and dishonour, praise and blame, are alike our lot: we are the imposters who speak the truth, the unknown men whom all men know; dying we still live on; disciplined by suffering, we are not done to death; in our sorrows we have always cause for joy; poor ourselves, we bring wealth to many; penniless, we own the world' (NEB).

Ideas are well-entrenched on the shop floor. When 'the Church' is referred to in conversation it is the Church of England complete with mothers' meetings, beaky-nosed effeminate vicars, tweedy spinsters and the annual sale of work. As the authors of *God's Frozen People* so aptly pointed out, they see God as a sort of Supremo after which come the bishops followed by the clergy and lastly the people split into two groups; magistrates, kings and governors on one side; dustmen, shopkeepers and plumbers on the other. The well-defined denominational categories which are so familiar to the initiated are largely unknown or ignored on the shop floor. The 'C. of E.' is a handy umbrella under which all the 'lesser brood' are conveniently sheltered.

There are catalogued questions – traditionally insoluble – which are invariably hurled at the Christian at some period of his pilgrimage through the workshops – 'Where did Cain get his wife from?', 'Did Adam have a navel?' (this last is calculated to deal a devastating blow at the very heart of Christian theology). Then there are the emotive questions 'Why does God permit wars/train disasters/road accidents/thalidomide babies' etc. etc. Thumbing through the pages of the New Testament to give scriptural answers will not, generally speaking, convince the critics because the Bible as a standard of reference is in dispute ('The Bible is mistranslated/full of contradictions/ fairy tales').

Gamesmanship plays a big role in these dialogues and the Christian is generally on the defensive and a 'loner'. He is dealing with organizational man, men in groups – something quite different from the earnest enquirer genuinely perplexed by legitimate doubts. These debating sessions are a critical test for the believer and any show of impatience, arrogance or ill-humour on his part will be immediately challenged and he will be subjected to a further fusillade of loaded questions – 'You aren't supposed to lose your temper, are you?' 'Aren't you supposed to turn the other cheek?'. This verbal sniping can be turned to good account by patient humouring and honest answers. Even the most antagonistic questioner melts before the calm and reasoned attitude of the Christian apologist!

Witnessing on the shop floor is sometimes a demoralizing business and one is tempted to maintain a tight-lipped silence when obdurate voices are raised against the Church and its institutions. Usually, however, it is only when the spectacular pronouncements and the arresting personalities make the news headlines that it is possible effectively to witness.

Dr John Robinson (one-time Bishop of Woolwich) and Dr Billy Graham have something in common for their respective messages percolated down to the shop floor and captured the imagination of the men, and the common denominator which unites them is the audacity, the freshness, the compelling force, the original presentation of their respective messages. Perhaps the Bishop takes first prize for his success against unimaginable odds, for his wordy wilderness *Honest to God* was eagerly seized by a highly vociferous and publicity-wise group – the doubt-mongers and 'new thinkers' of TV Press and radio. Dr Robinson for good or ill made Christianity a serious talking point on the workshop floor. Religion became sensational when a bishop of the Established Church decided to kick over the traces and publicly declare something my workmates had always believed to be true – that God wasn't 'out there'. *Honest to God* was soul-talk popularized. The good bishop admitted in his book *The New Reformation?* that he had not realized *Honest to God* might be a bestseller; otherwise, he suggests, he might have written it differently. So be it. Having demolished the traditional concept of a 'God out there' we are left with a vacuum which must be filled, and the complaint of an older theologian that 'no man cared for my soul' is still valid – although having canonized doubt the area of perplexity surrounding David's heart-cry is considerably widened.

The Earls Court Crusade of June '66 generated an intense interest in the workshop, but at the outset the value of Dr Graham's message was vitiated by what appeared to be the artificially manufactured 'Graham personality cult' and the irrelevant side issues. The lunch break discussions ranged around the £300,000 cost to promote the Crusade and how much of this money was being siphoned off into the pockets of Dr Graham and his team, and 'what a soft job he has' was the general opinion. (After the Crusade the hot debating point was what was to happen to the £54,000 'profit'!)

The Crusade was regarded as a panic measure on the part of the Church to shore up the collapsing ramparts of the dwindling congregations or perhaps just a gimmick to catch up with the times. The slick publicity organization and streamlined planning, the two thousand voice choir and TV city link-ups were regarded cynically and suspiciously and the charge of 'emotionalism' by some sections of the Press and TV all combined to produce in the minds of the workshop men the picture of a spiritual jamboree to be 'enjoyed' if one preferred that kind of entertainment. In vain I argued that as a Christian I had *been* to Earls Court and had known more emotionalism when overtime had been stopped for a few weeks than ever I had experienced at the Crusade. Again, I pointed out that organization and planning were vitally necessary for coping

66

with the huge crowds, and publicity was a means whereby people were made aware of what was happening. Regarding the question of finance I told them that neither Billy Graham nor any members of his team took a penny of the £300,000 and that he had publicly repudiated the personality cult. 'We have better local preachers in Moortown,' I explained, 'and Billy Graham has publicly stated that his gifts as a preacher are limited.'

' 'Ow about that 300,000 quid?'

'I've already explained, he doesn't take a cent' – and this was greeted with loud guffaws.

But it was hardly surprising that these unimaginative, dour men regarded the Crusade in these harsh terms for in 1961 when Dr Graham preached at the Municipal Sports Ground in Moortown – less than half a mile away from the works – hardly a handful of men bothered to go and hear what he had to say: after all, he spoke during the lunch hour break and they preferred to play crib in the canteen.

The committed Christian who enjoys the cut and thrust of debate will find plenty of scope for his talent in the shop-floor debates which range over the whole spectrum of human affairs. Sport, telly, sex, politics are the starting-off points and they include subsidiary and related items – religion, pools, holidays and pay. The telly with its instant opinion, nicely packaged and easily assimilated, is a kind of Urim and Thummim pronouncing infallible judgment on flashpoint topics – apartheid, the bomb, birth control and the pill. To protest a minority view on such occasions as for instance the death of Pope John engenders a peculiar kind of social ostracism. At that particular time the Cell concurred with the popular view that he was 'a good man' but drew the line when the eulogies became too lush, making the point that the communion he represented and the status he enjoyed were quite definitely unscriptural. This view exposed us to the charge that we were unchristian, narrow, biased and unbearably bigotted. To attempt to explain Reformation principles at such a time would have been to waste one's breath.

The Lord's Day Observance Society is another favourite chopping block although one may detect a grudging admiration for the pugnacity and vitality with which it propagates the cause of Sabbath observance.

In this uninhibited atmosphere of free discussion, the temperature towards the evangelical position varies from a freezing apathy to a white-hot hostility and it is easy for the Christian to become cynical and worldly-wise. One of the most disheartening features of workshop evangelism is the obvious lack of a sense of need on the part of the men. 'Need' is a dirty word and is connected with the 'evil thirties' and the means test, the grabbing and the grind of economic stagnation. This area of Moortown was badly hit with unemployment between the wars and there is still a working generation which remembers the snake-lines waiting for their dole outside the labour exchange. To tell a man he 'needs Christ' is to invite a prickly reflex of resentment. We live in an age of affluence and the only need that exists is the necessity of keeping up with the Jones's but when 'planned obsolescence' invades the sphere of moral values everybody gets hurt – including the Jones's.

Spiritual need is an admission of failure – and failure too is an unclean word. This is an age of *success*, technologically, socially and economically, and a failure is a misfit in a well ordered society. The Christian message begins essentially on a clarion note of failure and need. This is the basic teaching of the Fall, and man's pride is the first bastion in his nature that must buckle and, ultimately, collapse. Christianity diminishes and scales down man's fallen, egocentric nature and in this age, perhaps more than in any other, Christianity with its accent on the centrality of the work of Jesus Christ on the cross is a totally unacceptable and unpalatable way of life, the very antithesis of the spirit of the age.

The notion that 'change' is necessarily and intrinsically good is also a fallacy of the times – although this view is not always

68

shared on the industrial front. The introduction of work study methods and the consequent upheaval of time-honoured practices, restrictive and otherwise; the internecine fighting and feudings within the Unions, particularly in regard to lines of demarcation and membership; all these *may* produce smouldering resentment and ultimately provoke industrial action. But apart from these there is an agitation, an irritant difficult to define, intangible to understand, but nevertheless a very real malaise affecting the worker in industry. We may have to probe deeper to discover the reasons behind the 'kangaroo courts' the jungle law and wildcat strikes. 'The Union' gives a semblance of respectability and authority for those attitudes and actions which in any other context would be thoroughly reprehensible – even criminal – and inconsistent with civilized standards of behaviour. Men who are occupied in the mechanistic drudgery of the assembly line feel that in the deadly repetitive nature of their work they are merely an extension of the machine. Long hours of overtime bring fat wage packets and help maintain a high standard of living; but affluence exacts a price, the grinding monotony of the work conditions them to an intangible, indefinable resentment against the society they themselves have helped to create. It is not difficult for a strike to be sparked off by a word of rebuke from a foreman and a compound of fear and frustration will ensure that it snowballs.

There will be occasions when the Christian will have to nail his colours to the mast or else wound his spirit and compromise his conscience; in this regard he is peculiarly susceptible to temptations outside the normal sphere of Christian experience. Raising his hand with the rest when unconstitutional action is advocated, remaining silent when a fellow Christian is being castigated for refusing to join the Union on account of his personal convictions, yielding to the subtle pressures of the minority groups ...

Isolation, misunderstanding, embarrassment – these are some of the less vicious side-kicks he may be expected to encounter on the shop floor. Christianity may be patronized, ridiculed or politely ignored when it wears its clerical grey and is propagated in terms suggestive of a clerical grey respectability. Christianity in dungarees, however, represents a threat to the villainy of the minority groups and their vociferous disregard for established codes of conduct; indeed, it would seem that in many cases it is the *only* threat; Union leadership at national level shows a marked reluctance to grasp such nettles as the 'M6 Cabinet' and its infamous canteen convocations.

8. The Hard Cases

One comes across some hard cases. In a large nationalized industry where all sorts of men can be readily absorbed, there is always a tight nucleus of social misfits which does not conform to any regular social pattern. With these men the Christian's open ear may be more appreciated than the spoken word. Job's comforters were not altogether wrong in sitting mute before their afflicted friend seven days and seven nights. There is a good deal of spiritual therapy in allowing men to unfold their difficulties and problems to a sympathetic listener. There is a time to speak and a time to refrain from speaking and provided we are willing the Lord will grant us wisdom to differentiate.

Joe Busted was nearing retirement. He was a familiar figure in the works for 40 years. Except for minor changes due to reorganization he had trundled his four-wheeled barrow between 5 Shop and the various stores, carting nuts and bolts and other supplies. The only concession made to Joe in the mammoth BR reorganization plan was to substitute solid rubber wheels on Joe's barrow for the iron ones. This, according to Joe, was sheer folly for it made his task much harder. Joe's barrow was liberally sloganed and laboriously chalked with 'L' signs and 'Danger: Keep Clear' notices. Joe himself had boldly scrawled in streaky grey paint 'Keep off. Joe's Barrow. For 5 Shop Scrues Only!' When his barrow was not in use, Joe secured it by a long length of chain heavily padlocked. The unauthorized use of other people's barrows was a major bone of contention in Joe's mind.

The men named him 'Blossom' because he seldom smiled

and his outlook on life seemed perpetually wintry. His taciturn manner and the solitary nature of his job made me wonder what kind of man could have managed to go through the soul-destroying routine day in day out for 40 years. I spoke to one of the older hands about Joe and he volunteered the information that Joe had not always been withdrawn.

'Real lively character was Joe 'afore the war, but then 'is lad got killed at Cassino – at least, they found no trace of 'im. Joe never got over it. 'E was off work nearly 12 months after they notified 'im.'

A few weeks after this conversation I happened to spot Joe pulling his barrow up the yard. Characteristically his feet were splayed in a slow, measured gait, his head wedged into his shoulders against a biting wind and his arms extended behind him pulling the long handle of his barrow. He stopped momentarily and looked up as the first slivers of a heavy down-pour began to fall. Having satisfied himself as to the pointlessness of getting drenched for a few screws that the shop did not need anyway, he pulled his barrow under the sheltering roof of the car park. I followed him.

'Shocking weather!' I murmured conversationally as we stood in the darkening afternoon watching the widening puddles in the badly laid concrete and listening to the dismal metallic clatter of the rain on the tin roof.

He stared moodily into the nebulous reaches of the brick wall opposite. Thinking that he had not heard me I continued to chatter inconsequentially. At length he turned and in the jargon of the shop floor swore three times and said softly, 'Dry up!'

I dried up and evidently feeling that his spiky retort was perhaps too unkind Joe tried to make amends.

'It *is* rotten weather,' he said, 'it's *awful*. All the – rain seems to – well fall on this – place.' His sentence was punctuated with blasphemies which ricocheted in my sensitive brain. My acquaintance with him had been slight, but now he began to open up.

'Have you far to go to your home at knocking-off time, Joe?'
I asked.

'Nah. I live in Bullrose Street. Know it?'

'Yes.'

'They're pullin' 'em all down to make way for that new road. Always – well pullin' places down and never doin' owt about stickin' owt up in the empty space. Two years, they say, 'n then we'll be outed. Me and the missus 'ave lived there all our married life. It's only a small place. There ain't no bathroom 'n the lav is shared with next door; still it's what you're used to ain't it? I mean, we bought it as a sittin' tenant – cheap. In two years' time when the corporation buy it 'spect we'll only get 50 quid.'

'But they'll rehouse you Joe in a nice bungalow – all mod. cons too!'

'A bungalow would be just the job – for the missus. She's got heart trouble. The doctor's given me a paper to 'and over to the gaffer every time I 'ave a day or two off to look after 'er.'

'How long has she had a heart complaint?'

'About the time the lad got killed.'

'The lad?'

'Yes. Our Ken. 'E got killed at Cassino. The missus 'as never been the same since. Every night for years she's left the back door unlocked at night in case 'e came 'ome unexpected like. She keeps 'is room all ready for 'im – you know? 'Is civvy clothes, books, records – all 'is *own* things. I've tried to tell 'er and explain but she still thinks it's all a bad mistake 'n one o' these fine days 'e's goin' to breeze in like . . . We went to Italy six years on the run during the annual 'oliday – on the free pass you know? An' visited the place where they said 'im an' 'is mates were killed. But now we're knockin' on 'n the missus can't stand the long journey.'

There was an awkward silence while he fumbled in the inside pocket of his jacket and proudly showed me a crumpled photo of Ken in his army uniform. 'It ain't a good likeness,'

73

Joe said regretfully. 'It was taken on his embark. leave before 'e went abroad.'

'Do you believe that death is the end or do you feel you'll see him again?' I asked as I handed back the photograph. Once again, a blank uncommunicative stare was his mental range-finder as he carefully framed his answer.

'Oh, I dunno. I – well don't – well think so . . . ' and the oaths were repeated with impatient intensity as he bitterly continued ' . . . it ain't – well fair, there don't seem no sense in a – young bloke bein' – well killed by a lump o' – useless metal like these 'ere bolts; it just ain't right,' and then he suddenly flashed his eyes into mine and said emphatically, 'I know you're a churchy bloke. I go to church – once a year!'

'Remembrance Sunday?'

'Nah! – *my* remembrance Sunday, when Ken got done in, that's when I go . . . ' and the words trailed off in a barely suppressed sob.

I stood there feeling that this was one of those moments of truth not covered by those 'Personal Worker's Manuals' but at length quietly explained that God has also suffered in the Person of His Son at Calvary and this is the only explanation of the whole of human sorrow in the finality of things.

'But there was an Easter, Joe' I said, 'and even though I stand on the outside of your bitterness I know Someone who can enter into your sorrow and lift the cloud. I'm going to pray for you and your missus, Joe – and I know others too who will also pray for you!'

His eyes were luminous and had taken on a softer look. 'Thanks for promisin' to pray for me an' my missus. It ain't self-pity y' know.'

'I know that, Joe; it'll be a privilege to remember you in prayer.'

'I gotta go; they'll be wonderin' where I've got to . . . ' and Joe continued on his journey, a war casualty with a wound only the Great Physician can heal.

And then there is Albert Skemp. Albert is a chargehand over the labourers in 4 Shop and he is in his early fifties. His ruddy complexion is a glowing advert for that part of the shire where he lives in a small village, a fair distance from the smoke and grime of Moortown. He is a cheerful personality and well liked by the men who work under him – a rare combination as chargehands go.

I had not known him long before I spoke to him about Christianity. He shattered my confidence at the outset by holding his right hand in a kind of Nazi salute, half-closing his eyes and shaking his head and reminded me that 'an ounce of experience is worth a ton of theory.'

'What do you mean?' I asked.

'You talk about Christ suffering on the cross; I accept that – but there's an awful lot of suffering in the world and it isn't remote either. I mean, it's not a thousand miles away; it's right here in these works.'

And he began to unfold his story in short staccato sentences.

Albert had two sons, each in a different mental hospital. Kevin, the eldest is now thirty years old and has been an inmate since he was seven.

'We first found out he was poorly, like, when we had a letter from his schoolmaster saying he was backward,' he explained. 'I went up to the school to tear a strip off the headmaster, but it was true, Kevin wasn't like other lads. I blame the District Nurse; prolonged birth, that's what I put it down to. Well, he went to a special school until he was 14 and then he was transferred to Paxwright Hospital. He's a grand lad. We have him home every Saturday. John, my other boy, was born that way – you know?' I nodded reassuringly. 'Well, I put his trouble down to the fact that my missus fell when she was carrying him. He's 25 and has only been an inmate for three years. He got too much for the missus to handle.' Albert paused and furrowed his brow, 'It's a funny thing,' he went on, 'but that lad would talk to *animals*. I had two goats and at night he'd go into their den and talk to them in the dark. Same with cows. They'd sit there chewing the cud and young John would sit there with them, contented as you please. Poor John, we had to take him away from the last place. The nurse said he was getting sexy – you know – he'd put his arms around her waist. But he wasn't. John is just naturally affectionate and wouldn't harbour an evil thought in his heart.'

'How has your wife taken all this?' I asked gently.

'Oh, the missus has heart trouble. She's always on about the fact that if she hadn't fallen, John wouldn't be where he is today. Gets on her nerves – you know? Another thing, I've got big trouble on my hands at the hospital where John is. They've been beating him up – that's getting on my missus's nerves!'

'Beating him up?'

'Yes. It's driving my missus round the bend. Every night when I get home she's on about it. She's got arthritis in her legs – that don't help. Many a night I get my own dinner because she's crippled up with pain. Winter nights are the worst; they're long and dark and she don't seem to be able to snap out of her depression.'

'Have you had a visit from the minister of any church?'

'No. It wouldn't do much good would it?'

'Do you believe in God, Albert?'

'Course! Always have. But I don't go to church. I've got no time. After sorting the missus out and looking after the lads – I have 'em home on Sundays – there's not much time left.'

'You don't blame God – I mean – you aren't bitter in any way?'

'No. It's just life; the fruits of life, bitter fruits. It's – it's fate; you can't *blame* anybody,' and Albert fumbled and groped for words to express himself. 'We both love our lads. They've brought a lot of joy into our lives. Even the missus says that. These blokes who talk about putting mental defectives down the line like dumb animals don't know what they're talking about. They ought to ask *us*. Kevin and John love us and we love them, and after all you can't get beyond that, can you?'

And I had to agree. Love might not solve human problems,

76

but it does help people to bear them.

Members of the Cell often see Albert around the works and they chat with him about life in general. The men who work with him say he never mentions his domestic circumstances, but he is not so circumspect with Bert, Tom and the rest of us. He gives us an unsolicited report on his wife's and sons' progress and we in turn give him a sympathetic ear and the assurance of our prayers.

I often marvel at such men who in the midst of frightful personal tragedy are surprisingly resilient and seem to draw on a secret source of moral courage and strength; such men give little outward indication of being affected by their experience.

Albert does not identify himself with the Church except in the loosest possible way, but in his circumstances – which he would never regard as tragic – the Church must be identified with him. This is Christianity witnessing in rubber slippers and reaching men whose personal experience of life's dark imponderables clouds their view of orthodox evangelical methods.

But on the shop floor one also comes in contact with spiritual casualties; those whose experience in the Church has left them disillusioned and dissatisfied. Men like Peter.

Peter Grain was a young entrant for the sandwich course apprenticeship. His family lived in Kenya, where his father worked for a shipping agency. Peter's parents wanted him to have the best education they could afford so he spent the formative years of his life in England, first at a prep. school and then at a public school. However, academic studies were not Peter's metier; he had a practical bent and wanted a future in engineering. Consequently he was entered as a 'privileged' apprentice on a sandwich course on British Rail.

Moortown with its ugly sprawling industrial area, its perpetual smoke haze and endless corridors of ugly, dull, flat and featureless little houses dismayed Peter. He could not help contrasting the beauties of Somerset, where his public school

77

was situated, with the grimy industrial wasteland which properly belong to the nineteenth century. His digs were in Ponsonby Avenue and he was the only boarder. Mrs Gulch, his landlady felt that she had made the grade at last when her 'paying guest' spoke in such 'posh language' and really knew what fish knives were for. She was a widow and doted on Peter. He had appealing blue eyes and always wore a rather perplexed and apologetic look. On the rare occasions when he did smile, it always seemed rather lopsided. He was so polite and had such a distinctive air of class that the childless Mrs Gulch tended to lavish more attention on him than would otherwise be expected.

In the works Peter was regarded with a compound of suspicion and amusement. With his politeness, baby features as yet unshaven, unassuming manner and fastidious attention to details of dress – all packaged in the cultured accent of his public school – Peter was mercilessly lampooned. The very fact that he spoke *differently* aroused in some of the men a latent resentment: he was 'toffee nosed', and 'a snob'. Somehow, Peter felt that he must apologize for being what he was. He explained that his father had gone out to Kenya just after the end of the last war. They had lived in Romford where his father worked as a draughtsman and after he had completed six years wartime service in the army, he had decided to strike out for a new life in Kenya and had done very well ...

Peter was introspective and worried a good deal about his problems – his studies and relations with other people. He was most sensitive to the ill-conceived jokes and vicious witticisms of some of the men. They ragged him about his angelic features and mouthed their obscene platitudes daily in his ears. They sniped at him from behind the secure ramparts of their working class solidarity and salaciously jibed about the imagined facts of life in the murkier backwaters of the English public school system. Peter had no defence against all this. Another disconcerting factor which troubled him was his uncontrolled blushing when his face would rapidly change from a normal rosy pink to a beetroot red in a few seconds; this caused great amusement to his tormentors.

Not all the men reacted to Peter in this way. Some of them put themselves out and tried to help him during the six months he spent in the workshops but Peter did not make friends easily, the local dialect confused him, 'tha's' and 'wunner's', the 'surrey's' and 'cud'na's'.

It was no better at the Technical College. With a characteristic sense of discipline and conscientious regard for his studies, he worked extremely hard, but in his relationship with the other students there was a sense of isolation, a protective wadding of ultra-reserve which it seemed impossible to unravel. Lonely, hypersensitive, Peter was ripe for the psychiatrist's couch ... then the Church stepped in. One of his fellow students at the technical college succeeded in inducing Peter to go to a Youth for Christ rally and for the first time since coming to Moortown, Peter felt a certain kinship with the local people, especially the younger elements of the church fraternity. They invited him to their homes and they were not in the least embarrassed when he lapsed into his habitual silences. His gauche attempts to talk about things he thought *they* might be interested in were sympathetically handled and the cocoon of self-conscious frigidity gently began to fall away – not entirely, but sufficient to dispel the image in Peter's mind that he was a social misfit. At last, the Christian hospitality he had received and the atmosphere that had been generated massaged the inert spiritual desires in Peter's heart and one night, after a coffee squash in someone's home, Peter underwent a spiritual crisis and he invited Christ to come into his heart. Not that this momentous event made much outward difference to his life, but certainly a genuine transformation had taken place in his heart.

Life now began to assume a more friendly aspect, the ogre of his own inadequacies which had towered over his waking moments and shadowed all his activities now began to diminish, he had gained a new confidence and discovered a new dimension of social relationship in the church; here, it seemed, lay the answer to all his problems. Christ was a living Personality and he had come into contact with ultimate reality.

When his second spell in the workshops began there was a marked difference from the Peter we had known six months before. Previously, the overtures by members of the Cell to establish a rapport had failed miserably, but now Peter was far more approachable and he had lowered the barriers guarding his real personality. We conversed freely about his family in Kenya and he confided his hopes and fears. Peter had never really known family life, his holidays had been spent with an aging relative in Dorset and he confessed that he used to look forward to these periodic visits with bleak dismay. The sepulchral house, the cats, the rich, feeble old lady who was his grandmother continually harping about his father's misspent youth. The things we in the workshop took completely for granted – the family as an integral unit, an institution – Peter had never known.

Mrs Gulch with her pandering and indiscriminate favours had only served to sharpen his awareness of what he had missed, for he was now on the threshold of manhood and the years of his boyhood were lost. A less sensitive personality might have shrugged off this sense of estrangement and loss but Peter could not overcome the fractures in his own nature. Morbid introspection and a gloomy preoccupation with the mechanics of studying to make the grade in exams had been superimposed on what fundamentally was a happy disposition.

Now everything had changed: he had friends in the workshop and at the Technical College. The church which he attended provided an outlet for his social and recreational activities as well as his spiritual yearnings. He brought a motor scooter, played badminton in the winter and tennis in the summer. His boyish good looks and natural charm romantically attracted the impressionable young ladies of the church and soon he was indulging in mild flirtations.

But then, some of the young zealots of the church decided that it was high time that Peter took cognizance of his Christian responsibilities. They urged him to begin a course in learning how to memorize scripture passages and provided him with memory cards to start him off. Peter conscientiously spent 15 minutes every morning at this task. 'Meetings' now assumed a major significance in his life, the incubation period during which he was introduced into the Christian community was now over; during that period no one had suggested that he was in the first stages of spiritual declension if he missed a Bible study because of exams but now, eyebrows were raised and he was asked 'how did he expect to grow in grace if he wasn't fed on the proper food?' Steeling his naturally reticent disposition he attempted to make amends and show the others that he really *was* converted, that his spiritual experience really meant a great deal, so he stood in busy thoroughfares handing out tracts and invitations to meetings. Every nerve in his body seemed to disintegrate and he uncontrollably blushed when with faltering hand he timidly proffered his slips of paper to passers-by.

He was told that he *must* testify, he *must* tell others of what 'great things God had done for him' and Peter, sensing that his experience was invalid or insufficient to measure up to these demands became miserably perplexed.

He prayed. Oh! How he prayed! A horrible guilt complex now began to emerge, he spoke to the minister and the good man urged him to attend as many meetings as he possibly could: 'backsliding begins with slack abiding' he told him with a canny smile. The younger members of the evangelistic 'action group' at the church told him that Satan was an arch deceiver and a master strategist who recognized Peter's weak points and the only way to defeat Satan was to read the Bible more diligently, pray more fervently, testify more frequently, attend the meetings more regularly.

Peter, grappling with the complexities of technical engineering with a brain already blunted with too much thinking, was lamentably falling down on his studies. He was sleeping badly and Mrs Gulch with unnerving fussiness was watching his every move. His current girl friend was becoming very possessive and gushingly talked about 'their' future, and in Kenya political developments were taking place creating uncertainty for the European minority.

Peter brooded a long time over his latest crop of worries before finally deciding on a course of action and when he made up his mind, he acted with deliberation and characteristic dignity. First, he wrote a letter of resignation to the church secretary cutting himself off from all organized activity, and then he wrote a courteous letter to his girl friend explaining his reasons why he felt they should sever their relationship. He gave away his small collection of religious books which in his initial enthusiasm he had collected, and finally he gritted his teeth and one Friday night, after his supper cheese and cocoa, he told Mrs Gulch he was leaving having found other apartments.

After this minor social earthquake the minister and young zealots at the church sadly shook their heads and chatted about another promising young man who once 'ran well'; Peter's young lady pouted her lips and was heard to remark that she'd always known he was unstable but not *that* unstable! Mrs Gulch soon forgot Peter for he thoughtfully provided her with another boarder, more hardened to Mrs Gulch's benignity but equally appealing to her in his helplessness.

Peter, with two other engineering students, moved into a flat where they lived on curried beans and gargantuan Saturday night fry-ups. He still retained his classic dignity and charm but he was a much different Peter; we had known two Peters, Peter before his conversion and Peter after his conversion, and now there was another change. There was an undertone of cynicism in the new Peter's conversation and his slightly embarrassed aloofness had given way to calculated sophistication. The public school with its petty tyrants, its Spartan discipline, its character training, was clearly defined in the 'new' Peter's make-up. He was self-assured and self-reliant . . . Peter had come of age.

He passed his exams and now holds a top job on British Rail. Before he left Moortown to take a tidy leap up the ladder of success I spoke to him about his past. 'Is your Christian experience invalid? Was it a figment of your imagination, intellectual growing pains or an emotional discharge?'

'No,' he replied in all sincerity, 'it wasn't, but I was sandwiched between my studies and the high-pressured evangelism at the church. They were well intentioned, no doubt, but they failed to recognize that every person must be viewed against his particular background. Psychologically, I was at sixes and sevens and couldn't adjust myself to the particular environment they were creating . . . I go to church – periodically – but I'm not committed or involved in any way.'

Peter is a battle casualty and I often ask myself who is to blame for his present attitude towards the Church. Is he a product of unhealthy 'believism'? – but his conversion was genuine! Is it a passing phase where the edges of his commitment to Christ are blurred by the psychological and emotional pressures of a hard-pressed young student in an age of thrust and speed?

From his eyrie high on the plateau of a successful career, Peter often writes a brief, chatty letter, but always there is the scarcely perceptible motif of unsatisfied desire running through the lines. Looking back I wish there had been a younger Christian – one in Peter's own age group – who might have helped him. Peter was just like so many young men entering the industry and feeling their way towards establishing convictions in their lives, rather than merely forming opinions. Their difficulties are best appreciated by colleagues of their own age group. Here the younger Christian has a positive work to do. Communication between the age groups is very often much more difficult when one is 'thirty years on'! The bridge between the Christian faith and the unconvinced young man groping in a labyrinth of half-formed ideas is so often the young fellow who *knows* what he believes, and who *knows* in what direction his life is heading.

There is just time to tell you about Cobber. As long as he could remember, Cobber had smoked. But now it was a most distressing and inconvenient weakness because, together with his wife, Cobber had recently been converted. He had made successive attempts to conquer the habit without success and his misery was made complete by the knowledge that he had exposed his weakness to his mates and they seized every opportunity to remind him of his inability to give up. In half joking, half serious manner they pointed out how completely out of character it was that a *Christian* should smoke.

Cobber had tried every imaginable – and some hardly imaginable – methods to cut out the cigarettes. He had tried the psychological method of telling himself over a set period that on such and such a day he *would* break the habit, finally, absolutely, completely. His determination was as strong as his desire and he smoked twenty cigarettes a day until the fateful day arrived, D Day, Deprivation Day. Then the black depression would engulf him even before he rose from his bed, the gnawing hunger for nicotine would steadily oppress every nerve, and at work his mates would know that he had 'packed up' – again! It was a standing joke that 'Cobber packs up his fags three times every week'. With a fortitude born of high principled morality, Cobber would manage to hold out until the late afternoon and then he would furtively and feverishly search his pockets for a nub end with which, having located it in the lining, he would sneak off to the toilets and relieve his hunger for nicotine. He would return with a look of sublime satisfaction on his face and resume his labours. But his mates knew what had happened and unmercifully they would pitch into him, ' 'Im up there, 'E won't 'elp yer wiv the fags!' they would scoff, and Cobber, the dreadful implications of his action impacting upon him once again, that he had been a weak and a moral coward, would retreat into a private hell of morbid introspection.

He tried the shock treatment of abruptly stopping the habit after he had smoked the last cigarette in the packet but this was possibly the worst method of all for it was accompanied by a strong feeling of having cheated himself out of the last pleasurable – albeit dishonourable – sensation of savouring the *last*, the very *last* cigarette!

Cutting down his intake was also a well tried but futile method. His customary twenty a day would steadily be reduced to something like eight and this progress was achieved after painful exertion and nervous tension. But then, he would reason that it was not the number of cigarettes smoked but the act itself where the sin lay and so his revulsion of the vice would well up with fresh intensity until in no time, he had succumbed to temptation and was smoking his full quota and totally incapable of helping himself.

In every endeavour to conquer the habit he did not neglect to seek God's help in prayer but it seemed so futile, for the nagging persistency to indulge in the addiction proved too strong.

To the rest of the Cell, Cobber was an enigma and his transparent honesty did not help him to veil his vice. Although he did not smoke in public everyone knew he indulged. His fingers were nicotine stained, his breath was heavy with the smell of aniseed, cough sweets, eucalyptus and peppermints – pathetic attempts to camouflage his weakness – but always there was the unmistakable pungency of tobacco.

Once he went to a convention-type meeting and was afterwards invited to the minister's home for a cup of tea. Cobbers' lungs were bursting for a cigarette, there were other people present and he felt miserable and inadequate. He excused himself from the company and retreated to the toilet. Very carefully, he lit a cigarette and blew the smoke out of the window making quite sure that none was wafted into the confined space. His desire temporarily assuaged, he rejoined the company. But the secret could not be concealed – the undeniable odour of tobacco permeated the drawing room. Accusing eyes followed Cobber as he walked over to an armchair and sat down and Cobber knew that *they* knew. Of course, they had always known, but because Cobber had not been long converted the unwritten code regarding 'worldliness' which was strictly observed by members of Cobbers' church had been relaxed.

So, from this time, Cobber was regarded as somewhat of a black sheep of the flock and his addiction to the weed became something more than a spicy bit of gossip or a scarcely veiled plea in the prayer meetings to 'help our brother in his weakness'. However, in spite of cajolery, sincere and loving entreaties, and dark warnings of his bleak spiritual future if he did not break the habit, Cobber still persisted. On the surface it seemed that Cobber was not going to be morally bulldozed into abstinence and was merely being cussed and not a little untruthful when he protested that he was 'trying to pack up'. But at work he confessed to me that he was losing the battle and felt he was a substandard Christian and would always remain so. 'They keep knockin' me in the testimony meetings and in the sermons,' he said disconsolately, 'and if I say that I object, they'll say that I'm sensitive and it's conviction! Heads you win, tails I lose – you're beat every time!'

'What effect does this have on your wife, Cobber?'

'Oh, she's embarrassed but she never nags me about the fags, and somehow I can never light up in her company.'

'Don't you think you're battling on too many fronts? Your self-respect, your relationship with other people at work and at the church, the desire to puff at the fags, the web of deceit you've spun around yourself . . . ?'

'I agree with all you say but unless you've been really gripped by the habit, you've no idea what it's like . . . ' We held many such conversations but it was so obvious that as time went on the matter was assuming proportions entirely removed from the primary cause of the trouble.

Cobber's churchgoing gradually shaded off until it stopped completely and then he remained at home while his wife went. He spent his Sunday evenings at home following the evening service on TV. There was tight lipped disapproval of Cobber's behaviour and a melancholy reflection on the Demas-like

86

quality of Cobber's faith and there were even muted voices wondering whether he was truly converted or not, and there the matter rested for a few months.

The Cell clearly had a reclamation job on their hands, for Cobber no longer had his 'snap' with us as had been his previous habit. His workmates praised him for 'playing the man' and 'standing up for his rights' but Cobber's eyes betrayed his inner feelings; they looked strangely like Peter's must have looked on the night the cock crew; they were the eyes of a man who was terribly lonely and desperately unhappy.

I saw him one morning, a picture of utter dejection as with back arched over a pile of rivets he shovelled them into a trailer. 'Hello Cobber, how's things?' I enquired, half fearing what the answer might be. He straightened up and looked at me directly, 'I'm fine,' he said unconvincingly, 'but I'm finished with churchgoing. Oh, I believe everything you believe but I just can't go back, do you understand?'

'If you can't go back to *that* church, surely you can pick the threads up again at some other in the town?'

'It's . . . it's impossible, oh! it's not the fags, it's the *people* . . . ' and his voice wandered away with his eyes as I urged him to be more explicit. But it was no use, Cobber said he was a backslider and until something miraculous happened, he would remain so.

Cobber has been visited and prayed for; his wife, whom he loves dearly, he encourages to go to church and she confesses he is the best husband in the world. All the stock arguments, the tried and proven texts, all have been employed by different people over the years and the only concession Cobber has made is to visit the church at Harvest, Christmas and Easter. Then the red carpet treatment is afforded him and immediately the service is over, Cobber nips smartly outside and lights up while his wife apologizes for his speedy departure, his sensitivity to any kind of social atmosphere long since evaporated.

His wife loves him with a certain compassion and ascribes his lapse to human frailty – his. Cobber blames the stiff-necked pharisaical clique at the church who didn't give the ink on his decision card time to dry before they were peppering him with their moral grapeshot. And they, thankful that the offending leaven of worldly impurity is removed from the 'testimony' blame the world, the flesh and the devil.

And so to men like Cobber and Peter, disillusioned by their experience of the Church, as well as to the social misfits the Cell is also called on to extend a therapeutic ministry.

Epilogue

As I write, the night is full of sounds; the metallic jingle of steel on steel as shunting operations are carried out in the near-by rail yard; the frightening two-toned hoot of the giant diesel locos as the freight wagons are trundled into position; the heavy lorries as they speed along the A6 and the roar of the rocket motors on the test-beds of Moortown's giant aircraft works. The confusion of sounds confirms the scriptural truth that we are 'fearfully and wonderfully made', suitably conditioned to accept these decibelic horrors as the 'price of progress' – a blanket cliché which covers Bright Tom's place at a red brick university, sodium lighting on the main road, and the rising cost of living.

Most of the men who work in the rail works live on the sprawling council estates which skirt the industrial centre of Moortown. From the air these resemble immense spider's webs whose gossamer lines of uniform brick houses span outwards from the quick nerve centres of commerce – the Wimpy Bar, Woolworths, Boots, Barclays, Fine Fare.

The estate citizen lives in a world conditioned to the pill, pools, Coronation Street, pop, fish fingers, instant (telly) opinion, transistors, packaged soup, tanked tigers, holes with mint on the outside, lung cancer, Vietnam, vogue words and crazes. It is the same world which God so loved, the same world to which Paul was crucified, the same world which, according to St John, has been overcome by the Christian's faith. A far, far cry from the quiet hills of Galilee and its Sabbath calm but . . . the same world.

Two cultures meet on the shop floor; one is earthy, synthetic and ephemeral, the other is permanent and otherworldly. But too often the image portrayed of the Church is of an institution bedevilled by its own doctrines, always in a ferment and constantly reacting to crises thrust upon it by a world bitten by the Athenian bug of change for change's sake. Discussions concerning the 'God is dead' and 'Ground of our being' philosophy sounds strangely out of touch in a world unconsciously waiting to hear the voice of the prophet.

The Christian in the workshop is part of that prophetic voice and, like Thomas, the world is waiting to see the brand-marks of the cross in those who profess 'Jesus Christ is Lord'.

It will not always be easy to feel one is there because God wants one there. The majority of men perform boring and monotonous jobs, though in surroundings which have been made as congenial as possible, and their frustration and grumbling is infectious.

The temptation to slacken the taut guidelines of one's Christian testimony is always present. Compromise as a matter of expediency will seem an attractive solution in many situations where righteous indignation may be an expensive luxury – expensive in terms of the HP system of repayment; moral courage is paid for in the hard currency of ostracism and snide remarks. When temptation comes it will probably be in the form of bluff comradeship, and it will be the fellow who has helped you in the past and who has sympathetically listened to your account of the 'good news'. He it is who will ask you to clock his card so that he can be first out of the gates as he has to visit his sick mother in hospital and time is at a premium.

Swearing, working Sunday for a double time pay off, the right use of leisure/money/time – these are the more obvious issues which spring readily to mind. These will be easily answered when the crunch comes and there will be a mountain of helpful literature to advise.

It is the less obvious situations which will cause the warning bells to ring in your brain: you are sitting at the bench with your mates at snap time. A cheeky, good-natured fellow points to a voluptuous pin-up, digs you in the ribs, smirks and says, 'How'd yer like 'er, then?' There is a *double entendre* in the remark – it is deliberately phrased, and your answer – whatever it might be – will, to the men, have elastic sides. A month's ridicule has been fashioned on a hasty reply or an ill-considered remark.

Expediency as a working philosophy will be presented when old Jack, a nice, kindly man asks you to keep a lookout for the watchman as he lights his fag in a prohibited area, or some helpful soul sees you hurrying down the yard and tells you to ease up because he's already clocked your card (a serious wrong punishable at law in some cases). Once you accede in these ways and fall into line you will be accepted and should some weightier matter present itself in the future involving a definite stand on principle, you will be forcibly reminded of your previous defection.

It will be your barbed reply, your sarcastic rejoinder, your display of temper, your show of impatience which will be noted and acted upon by the men. Your views on the Christian's use of leisure time and whether Sunday observance is a Christian priority will not be half as important as the way you react in the crisis of an argument about whether Sam Grudge should have been given two days' suspension for swearing at the foreman.

But whatever the situation in which he may find himself involved, the Christian will invariably find others on the shop floor who own the name of Christ and who will sympathetically regard his problems as their own. They will readily appreciate his desire to be a 'workman that needs not to be ashamed' in all areas of life.

Blake, with rare insight, may have snared a vision of the New Jerusalem rising like a phoenix from the industrial ashes of the nineteenth century, but on a bleak Monday morning in October, when a razor east wind shaves the narrow streets adjoining the rail works of their litter and leaves and the buses disgorge their human cargo outside the main gates, the author will be forgiven if he does not share the poet's vision; perhaps Jerusalem was not built here, but there is every possibility that its stones have been quarried in such places!

Commentary and questions
for discussion

COMMENTARY ON CHAPTER 1

Unless it could be shown that the nature of the job created a strain on office staff if their hours were the same as the factory, a very strong case exists for removing this 'perk'. On the other hand, as a legitimate incentive to doing the job I suppose it is as valid as piece-work bonus on the shop floor. The problem of depersonalizing is, of course, a lot older than modern technological progress. In the old days factory employees were often known as 'hands'. I have known 400 sacked in one day, at two hours' notice. The constant reminder that man is made in the image of God and gets his dignity from this fact is the only adequate spur to proper treatment in any age.

The description 'soul-destroying' fits a job for one man and may be quite wrong of the same job in the hands of somebody else. For instance a man who dislikes teaching, but is stuck with it, will spend his days fighting 'the brats' while another teacher finds fulfilment in working with human beings. An ex-car-worker said to me 'When I was on the line I was making *cars*'. He did not see himself as merely putting the same nut and bolt in the same place on the same piece of ironmongery passing him on the conveyor belt.

A student I was accompanying round a car works said to me, 'If any of these men are going to Hell I shouldn't think they'd notice the difference'. I asked a man from the line to comment on this later, and he pointed out to the student that men on the job don't see it that way. They don't notice the noise and don't think of the job in a hostile way. This was an illustration of the fact that 'soul-destroying' is a relative term, depending on who is asked to do the job. Good management, respecting the dignity of its employees, will obviously make every effort to see that the men *know* what the company makes and why. Then those who want to can have an intelligent interest in the work they spend so much of their lives doing. Many men prefer a job where they know what is coming and don't have any worries.

Again, as Emil Brunner says, there is the dignity of *wages*. Good pay can give a job real value. The foreman in many works today is a very different official from the days when he got his promotion by buying other people pints. An earthquake shock travelled round one plant when the management announced tests for chargehands to see if they were foreman-material since the chargehand rank was to go. Now all foremen have to do a course in man-management and although I suspect that in smaller concerns things are much as of old, in bigger companies foremen either have a more managerial title or in other ways are being given a status indicative of their newly recognized importance.

Questions for discussion on chapter 1

1. Is the class distinction of salaried staff from shop staff unavoidable? Is it even desirable as an incentive?
2. What is a Christian attitude towards ambition?
3. If there will always be a need for the dirty and unskilled jobs to be done, how can those doing them be seen to matter and have dignity?

COMMENTARY ON CHAPTER 2

The stories of Bert, Tom, Jim and 'God's middle-man' George, underline that the Church is *already* in industry, wherever there are people who have met Christ in a personal way. Time and again Christians prove, with the Communists, that there is strength and a sense of direction to be had from meeting in the Cell. Where the Communist frequently scores over us, however, is that he doesn't only use the Cell for ideological instruction and mutual encouragement but also as a place where strategy is worked out, and his place in the factory related to wider issues in the country and even internationally.

The salt function of the Christian mentioned in the last chapter is that of the salt-cellar not the brine-tub. While to help others to be honest or more pure is a right thing to do, the salt needs applying in the shop-stewards elections and other TU offices. The Christian's responsibility to love his neighbour involves caring for his working conditions and wages as well. This is clear from Leviticus and James 5. Also he must be concerned to help prevent Union functions being subverted for undemocratic ends. I wonder how different the history of the ETU would have been if every Christian electrician had played his full part in that union's affairs?

Further, the Christian's effectiveness in witnessing to men of the calibre found among many TU groups will be greatly increased by his being *seen* to have a concern for the issues of justice which engross them. In fact, for many such men, the chances of hearing the gospel are greatly reduced, just because Christians so frequently opt out or are too busy running church activities to find time for working for their workmates.

Questions for discussion on chapter 2

1. Is there a danger that involvement in union affairs and other matters that Bert would call 'unspiritual' could weaken positive Christian witness?

2. Would you describe Tom's conversion as sudden?

3. Do you think it is significant that both these men were converted in informal free-church settings? Is liturgical worship a barrier to such people?

4. Do you think that other Christians should try to change Bert's outlook or is he more valuable to the Cell as he is?

COMMENTARY ON CHAPTER 3

The trouble is that the 'awkward squad' can become an excuse for the other Christians to do nothing about specific witness. Yet David Sheppard the present Bishop of Woolwich constantly testifies that he was won for Christ through a man who was prepared to lose his friendship by offering him the gospel. It is probably true that the cause of Christ suffers far more from silent Christians than from the odd bods. This is suggested by the success of Jehovah's Witnesses on the one hand, and, to some extent, the successful proselytizing by Communists on the other.

Without the word to explain it, the sacrament of a godly life can prove a hindrance to the 'Egyptians'. The true story is told of a man who went to a meeting and was converted. Returning to work next day he shared the experience with a colleague in the office. The man said he was glad and had been a Christian for many years. The new Christian replied, 'I've told people for years that if a fellow can be as good as you without religion I don't need it!' . . . so the other man's life, without the word of explanation, had become a barrier in his neighbour's path.

Questions for discussion on chapter 3

1. Can you witness for Christ without words?
2. How should the Cell cope with its awkward member?
3. Cecil was right about Donald Waterson being his brother. Was he wrong in what he did? If so, how?

COMMENTARY ON CHAPTER 4

For the Bible Christian as distinct from the New Testament one there can be no escape from the reality of God's justice. Righteousness in Isaiah has to do with treatment of the widow and the fatherless. The Psalms ring with the thought that God is the God of the poor and the weak and will vindicate them. When James calls rich men to howl over unpaid wages he is providing a New Testament parallel to what the Old Testament prophets had to say. When Paul tells the Colossian Christians to pay their slaves what is just and equal he is bringing a thought quite foreign to what was usual on the 'rights' of slaves. From Leviticus onwards the Bible argues for justice for the employee. Less often it also calls for the employee to work properly for his employer, the variant stress being due to their relative positions of power I suppose. The pietistic view, ('we have here no continuing city, we seek one to come'), perhaps more easily explained as the 'pie-in-the-sky' point of view, denies this stern element of justice in Old and New Testaments (but chiefly in the Old). Yet we have no right to press Sabbath observance on Old Testament grounds if we at the same time want to discard it on matters of social justice.

It would seem that Evangelical Christians ought *not* to be under-represented in the field of Trade Union leadership. Because of this biblical emphasis on God's character in the realm of justice the Evangelical cannot be a mere pietist or a quietist (*i.e.* we mustn't make trouble – 'Blessed are the peace-makers'). Jesus said He came to bring a sword as well as peace.

However, since God does not only speak about rights but also responsibilities the Christian may well find himself out of step with fellow-activists in organized labour. In that case, if he can't carry his point he merely loses at the next elections, a hazard which any officer faces anyway.

Questions for discussion on chapter 4

1. What is the Christian's basic position on trades union involvement?
2. Is the class struggle element in industrial relations inevitable?
3. What does the Christian member do when he disagrees with an official industrial action?

COMMENTARY ON CHAPTER 5

One may ask whether total 'integration' is just a goal of theorists and not the desire of either all the white-coloured or all the dark-coloured run-of-the-mill human beings. (Direct experience in a multi-racial community has convinced me of this.) One finds that Muslim people, for instance, badly want to keep their own patterns of community and worship. West Indians feel more at home with their own folk and have their own brand of humour and musical appreciation and so on. It may seriously be asked whether those pressing 'integration' are not in fact doing despite to the dignity and worthwhileness of our immigrant folks' own culture and thought-forms and way of life, and doing the same to our patterns as well. What seems to be needed is genuine respect for other nationalities' characteristics in a multi-racial society rather than the deliberate ironing out of differences by forced policies. This acceptance of the multi-racial society is, of course, much more delicate and potentially dangerous because it accepts people as they are rather than trying to engineer them into conformity.

The only reliable basis for race relations is the Christian doctrine that all humanity came from one common stock, that all its members are equal under God, that Christ died for all men everywhere and that all everywhere are answerable to God in the end. This is the only reliable way to secure both individual human dignity and value while at the same time preserving law and order and the just requirements of the indigenous nation.

Questions for discussion on chapter 5

1. Why do you think that the workers described in this chapter were prejudiced against coloured immigrants?

2. Do you think that different groups should be encouraged to preserve their own customs and cultures now they reside in this country?

3. Do you think it was a good or bad move that Thomas' friends left to form their own black congregation?

COMMENTARY ON CHAPTER 6

When speaking of the standardization of council house architecture it is worth remembering that the people inside the houses are *not* standardized. The style of decoration will vary a lot. The things which get priority also vary. Surprisingly perhaps there will be one home where the cocktail bar in the corner is the 'centrepiece'. For another the greenhouse down the garden is much more important and for others the car outside the front door is the top thing. Some go in for pigeons and others for budgies. Some go in for unusual fireplace arrangements while others display the mass-produced but striking window-sized 'mural' type views in full colour. It sometimes happens that men appear more 'standardized' at work than they really are when seen in the home context. This knowledge may help perhaps, when we are trying to be alongside a fellow-worker.

When rubbing shoulders with the *Morning Star* distributer or the 'poor man's Malcolm Muggeridge' it is worth remembering that there is a Christian philosophy of life also. The Bible isn't only about being saved, although this is of top priority in view of its eternal importance. It is also about man's origin and it has plenty of political commentaries (see almost any of the Old Testament prophets or Christ's stand before the religious leaders, and Herod and Pilate). Sometimes witness to Bible principles about social situations leads men to see the relevance of Christ, something they may not otherwise realize outside of some pressing personal need. Thus a leading trade union official who became a member of his local Baptist church said to his Anglican industrial chaplain who didn't preach the gospel so much as try to interpret industry and society in biblical terms:

'I wouldn't be where I am now if you hadn't first caught my interest by relating religion to life.' That had evidently been pre-evangelism.

Questions for discussion on chapter 6

1. Is the author unfair towards the nominal Christian on p.50?
2. Why is it important for every Christian to have an understanding of doctrine?
3. 'The Bible isn't only about being saved.' Do you agree. If so, what else is it about?

COMMENTARY ON CHAPTER 7

One occasionally meets people who have opted for teaching or 'the church' because they could no longer stand the tensions of 'the world'. People for whom big-business with all its cynicism or the Unions with all their naked party-interest have made commerce or industry uninhabitable for the idealistic. However, the blunt truth is that in teaching or the church they are in fact financed by the products of industry and commerce since their callings are not in the economic sense productive.

Some of the practices in industry are a challenge to Christians to change the system. Industrial democracy or *The Responsible Company* outlined by George Goyder in his book of that name* remind us that things do not have to stay the way they are. While restrictive practices and the scrounging mentioned in this chapter seem impossible to eradicate short of an economic crash in the country or political revolution, the truth is that Zeiss-Ikon of Germany have been practising responsible company techniques since 1886!

In 1967 the French Government under Charles de Gaulle published proposals for giving workers a stake in the profits of the firms that employ them. The plans apply compulsorily to all firms employing 100 or more persons. This could be a reason for the quieter history of French industrial relations in recent times. The British Economist Paul Bareau outlined the plans in the *Sun* newspaper for August 7th, 1967. George Goyder would argue for far more than profit-sharing and include also, worker-participation at director-level. This was

* (*Basil Blackwell, 1961*)

enforced in certain industries by the Allied Occupation on Germany after the last war. A German industrialist recently remarked 'It works excellently. Why don't you (the British) apply it to yourselves'. The Christian faced with practices in industry which offend his personal code needs to look deeper and ask if the *system* is conducive to honesty and fair-dealing and if it isn't then plainly the Christian should be one of the first to think about and work for changes.

Meanwhile, compromise is often unavoidable, where gang-work is the pattern, and where 'accepted practice' is not at all what the Christian might personally think is right. It would seem that he is not without biblical warrant for adjusting to the situation while not approving it. When Naaman said to Elisha that he would be bowing in the House of Rimmon (a false god), since his master leant on him, Elisha did not say, 'Give up the job' but 'Go into peace'. When Paul was asked to adjust to the Jerusalem situation and shave his head and keep a vow because of the Jews he did it. And he, the actual writer of Galatians in which the circumcision controversy is so thoroughly thrashed out, calmly took Timothy and circumcised him because of the Jews! So it would seem that where the issues are clear-cut and flagrant dishonesty is involved the Christian says No. But where 'accepted practice' is less than he would regard as right there is a case for adjusting to it and where the system has created the practice he has a responsibility to help improve the system. Lastly, to opt out so as to enter a more 'godly' situation may in fact merely remove the problem one stage since he will more than likely be living off the fruits of the system he has sought to escape.

It happened in the battle for Factory Reform waged by Lord Shaftesbury that a factory-owner opposed to the use of child-labour would have to use it because of the economics of the situation. However, he could and did fight by speeches, by finance and by publishing to change the system in the country and so make it possible to stop the thing he hated in his own works.

Questions for discussion on chapter 7

1. How can the Christian best prepare himself for the outward thrust of tea-break debate?

2. Do you agree with what the author says in the first paragraph of this chapter (p.58)?

3. Do you agree that humour is an indispensable part of the Christian's armoury?

4. Do you think people show any sense of need?

COMMENTARY ON CHAPTER 8

A lot has been said in recent years about the Church ministering to man 'in his strength' or 'man come of age'. Anybody who lives in the real world knows that this wonderful technological chapter in man's history is absolutely littered with casualties and simply to gear the church to man's pride in his achievements will in the end be a betrayal of humanity. It is as right today for the Church to be looking out for and caring about the people with heavy personal burdens as it ever was . . . and the need is maybe greater than it used to be.

Maybe the problems relating to Peter and Cobber had to do with the unfortunate turn of events which has found the Church a community of 'saints' instead of a community of sinners who know they are, and whom God is turning into saints. The unjudging spirit is not always easily come by in the Christian fellowship. We too often find ourselves in the Judge's seat which doesn't belong to us. Usually I suppose this happens because we are getting behind with the *personal* check-up. When the fellowship is the kind the elderly John refers to in his first epistle (1 John 1.7) it has to do with being in the light with one another with the Blood of Jesus Christ cleansing from all sin. Probably if Cobber knew the church fellowship which judged him over smoking as God knew them he wouldn't have felt quite so devastated over their apparent perfection, and they might together have shared their needs and weaknesses and prayed *for one another.*

Questions for discussion on chapter 8

1. It takes time to be a reliable and understanding friend to the Joe's and Albert's. In what way can we ensure that our active participation in affairs of the church does not limit our caring for our neighbour?

2. Did either Peter or Cobber find themselves in the sort of Christian community described by John in 1 John 1.4-10? What do you think were the good points in their environment and what were the things that hindered their maturity?

3. List the reasons why smoking is considered an undesirable habit in many Christian groups. Do you think in Cobber's case it was his inability to break with the habit that was the cause of his break with the Christian church, or was there a more serious reason?

4. Tell the group of one way in which you have experienced the liberating power of Jesus Christ. Do others feel accepted by you, just as they are, or do you expect everyone else to have exactly the same experience as you have had?

5. Do you agree with Peter's own diagnosis of himself as 'sandwiched'? What things do you think could have helped and what hindered his development into the freedom of the Christian life?

COMMENTARY ON THE EPILOGUE

The Home Help is asked by the client to fill time-sheets that she has been working when she has not. This is to secure continuity with the same house.

The civil engineer is expected to over-state the amount of concrete for the foundations because his boss says it is 'usual practice'.

The company director must turn a blind eye to the use of sex for the sale of his firm's wares debasing one of humanity's finest gifts for the sake of profit.

The television producer/writer must slant the programme a particular way or put in unnecessary titillation if there is to be hope of more work.

The journalist must sacrifice sensitivity to sensationalism in the interests of circulation.

The tycoon's minions must see the destruction of smaller people's means of livelihood in the interests of commercial empire.

The minister of religion must adjust the Bible's revelation to the limit he considers the people in his congregation will be prepared to stand, and soft-pedal from then on.

The schoolteacher must accept the pouring of educational funds into developing the potential of the 'A' level types, while the 'remedial' classes get less and less of the financial help which could provide the aids which could make more and more C and D stream strugglers into reasonably effective citizens. After all the school's image is at stake.

And so on and so on, in local government, in national politics, in medicine, in professional sport and any other human activity you care to name. These are the sorts of accepted practices we find.

On the shop floor it involves clocking-in, restrictive practices, and what some consider to be the legitimate scrounge. Right through society the Christian needs wisdom to discern where he must pay the price of being 'salt of the earth' and where to 'ask no question for conscience sake'. He has the equally difficult task of avoiding being a prig. Sense of sinnership and a sense of humour go a long way here.

Falcons – readable Christian books

On the Job
by Barry Palmer and David Durston – 20p

A simple, clear and concise introduction to the world of work—written for young Christians going into industry, but of great value to ministers, youth leaders and teachers who need to be able to advise them at that moment.

The World of Work

A CPAS filmstrip based on a chapter in *On the Job*; the price of £1.60 includes notes and discussion questions and a copy of the book.

The Case against Christ
by John Young – 25p

The author examines the case for the defence in a lively, easy-to-read style, answering convincingly many of the objections often made to Christianity.

God thoughts
by Dick Williams – 30p

'A devotional happening for the young-minded' - prayers and meditations, very much in the modern idiom by one of the authors of *The Gospel in Scouse*. More than 25,000 already sold in the UK.

Journey into Life
by Norman Warren

A very basic guide to becoming a Christian; *The Way Ahead* by the same author follows up in the same style, and *Directions* is 15 simple Bible study outlines on the basics of Christian belief. All at 5p.

write to the publishers for full list